super easy cookbook for beginners

super easy cookbook for beginners

5-Ingredient Recipes and
Essential Techniques to
Get You Started in the Kitchen

lisa grant

ROCKRIDGE
PRESS

Design: Christopher T. Fong
Editor: Vanessa Ta
Production Editor: Erum Khan
Cover photography © Marija Vidal, 2018
Interior photography © Hélène Dujardin, 2018; food styling by Lisa Rovick
Author photography © Andrew Maier, 2018

ISBN: Print 978-1-64152-033-1 | eBook 978-1-64152-034-8

TO JOHN, NICOLE, AND EDDIE.
I hope my cooking always brings
as much joy to you as it does to me.

CONTENTS

INTRODUCTION

I HAVE LOVED FOOD for as long as I can remember. I grew up in an Italian-Croatian family where Sunday dinner was the highlight of the week. This meal was more than just dinner—it was an event. It consisted of several courses, and many times we had our grandparents, aunts, uncles, and cousins over. The food was simple but delicious, and perfect for a crowd. I remember the big bowls of pasta and salad, roasted chicken, and tureens of chicken tortellini soup. Everything was served family style. Dinner often ended with pastries, cakes, or pies and a pot of freshly brewed coffee.

While I always associated Sunday afternoons with food, it was really about family, eating together, and laughing around the table. Good food does not mean fancy, expensive, or complicated. It is more about being delicious without doing a lot of work. The less work there is, the more time you have to enjoy the food with others.

Cooking has been my thing for years. I have always loved to read cooking magazines and cookbooks. But I was never a big fan of following recipes that had a long ingredients list or required ingredients that came from a specialty food store. When I read a recipe and see that it's longer than my son's high school English paper, I know that recipe is not for me.

When my children were young, meals were as fuss free as possible. Most nights I got dinner on the table very quickly. My grocery store trips were infrequent and had to be quick because I traveled with toddlers in tow. I made sure to keep the right ingredients on hand so I could prepare easy, simple food.

What I learned growing up is that mealtimes should be relaxing, with no stress involved. I learned how to make that true for me, and I wrote this book to show you how it can be true for you too. You may not have grown up in a family of cooks, and you may not have read all the recipes I have, but the truth is that it's easier than you think to make stress-free meals in your own kitchen.

In this book I'll guide you to cook lots of great food without lots of work. It contains a collection of recipes, all of which use only five main ingredients—there will be no long grocery shopping lists. The prep is minimal, too. You do not need any cooking experience to make the simple recipes in this book. Follow the instructions and you will be on your way to wonderful, worry-free meals.

The recipes in this book are similar to the ones that I have eaten over the years at those Sunday dinners. I have tweaked many of them so you can still make them when you're crunched for time, like I usually am. Cooking should be enjoyable, and if you have children, these recipes are easy enough that they can help you. There are recipes in this book that will allow you to get dinner on your table more quickly than leaving the house to pick up takeout.

This book contains:

- Easy five-ingredient recipes that are suitable for breakfast, lunch, and dinner. There are also snacks, desserts, and a chapter on sauces, dressings, and staples. The five main ingredients are not counting basic items you already might have in your pantry, like salt, pepper, and everyday spices. You will find out more on what should be in your kitchen pantry in the first and second chapters of this book.

- Recipes that are convenient and can be made in 30 minutes or less, one-pot or one-pan recipes, slow cooker recipes, and recipes that can be made ahead of time or stored in the freezer. I've also included recipes that accommodate dairy-free, gluten-free, and vegetarian diets.

- Lots of tips and techniques to make cooking simple. The first two chapters will equip you with everything you need to be successful in the kitchen. There will be more tips accompanying every recipe to guide you through the process.

- Recipes that contain whole ingredients, most which are not processed or premade. The ingredients you will be using are easy to find at your local grocery store, and you will eat fresh, wholesome food.

- Home-style favorites to feed your family. My family has enjoyed these recipes, and I'm sure yours will, too.

Chapter 1

Set Up Your Kitchen

BEFORE YOU START COOKING, you need some essential kitchen tools, necessary appliances, and staple ingredients to store in both your pantry and the refrigerator. I'll also give you some tips on shopping and storage, and ways to be efficient when making these recipes. With just a little preparation, you will be ready for this new cooking adventure. I want you to be relaxed and prepared so that you can enjoy cooking.

Welcome to the Kitchen

Get ready for your home to smell delicious! Your mouth is going to water when you see the recipes you're going to cook. While it's wonderful to have a big kitchen with lots of space, I've lived in several small apartments that had kitchens no bigger than a walk-in closet. My small kitchen table doubled as a work space and an eating area. No matter how big or small your kitchen is, it will be your space and you can cook great meals in it.

If you take inventory of your kitchen, you'll probably realize that you already have many of the basic kitchen necessities needed to cook everything in this book. Don't worry if you don't. Anything you need can be purchased in stores like Target or Walmart. And if you're really busy, you can buy everything online from places like Amazon.com. Once you have everything you need, make sure your tools and supplies are easily accessible so that you can use them whenever you'd like to cook.

The kitchen has always been my happy place, and I hope it will be yours, too. You'll get lots of satisfaction from making food for yourself and feeding others. Once you start cooking, you'll want to invite family and friends over for dinner. Be ready, though, because no one will want to leave your kitchen!

Gather Your Tools

The right tools and appliances can make your life super easy in the kitchen. There's no need to purchase fancy equipment, because the recipes in this book require a kitchen stocked only with simple items. This is what you need to get started. At the end of the list are a few optional appliances you might want to think about purchasing in the future or once you are a more experienced cook.

BASIC TOOLS

Bakeware: You'll need a few rimmed baking sheets (13-by-18 inches) for baked goods and roasting meats and vegetables. A ceramic casserole dish, an 8- or 9-inch square pan, a 9-inch glass or ceramic pie plate, and a 12-cup muffin tin are the other pieces of basic bakeware you'll need.

Box grater: This is a grater that has an open bottom, a handle at the top, and different-size grating holes on each side. You'll use it to easily shred or grate cheese, vegetables, and dry bread.

Can opener: A basic handheld can opener is all you need.

Colander: This is essential for draining the water from pasta and vegetables. I also use it to defrost ingredients like frozen shrimp.

Cutting board: One large board is sufficient. However, I like having one for cutting meats and poultry and a few others for cutting fresh produce. This makes it easy to keep any type of bacteria from raw meat away from the produce and other ingredients. I favor plastic cutting boards for meats and poultry, as they are dishwasher safe and clean up easily. I also love having a few small wooden ones to chop up herbs and produce.

Instant-read thermometer: This is a thermometer that's inserted into food to get an automatic temperature reading. It's a good tool to test the doneness of meats and poultry.

Knives: A 10-inch chef's knife and a 2- to 4-inch paring knife are essential for food prepping. Make sure to keep them sharp. You can take them to a hardware or kitchen store every year or so if they need to be sharpened. If your knives don't hold a sharp edge for that long, you can sharpen them monthly with a little handheld sharpener you draw the knife through. There is more information about the knives you will be using in the Master the Knife section of chapter 2 (page 12).

Ladle: This is useful for serving soups and stews.

Measuring cups and spoons: You'll need various-size cups and spoons to measure out both dry and liquid ingredients. They come in sets, so I recommend one set of each as well as a transparent measuring cup for liquids. Dry measuring cups are used for flour, sugar, and solid ingredients, while the transparent measuring cups are used for liquids and have a spout on the rim for easy pouring.

Mixing bowls: A set with three sizes should cover it all.

Pastry brush: This tool looks like a paintbrush and is perfect for coating foods with liquid ingredients, like barbecue sauce, as well as oiling or buttering a baking pan.

Parchment paper: This is my go-to tool for baking or roasting on a rimmed baking sheet. It's sheets of thin paper that you line your pans with to prevent foods from sticking, and it will make cleanup super easy. Be sure to buy the boxes of precut sheets. This way, you will not have to cut or measure the sheets, and they do not curl up the way a paper roll would. I buy them in my grocery store or on Amazon.

Peeler: Use this to remove the skin from fruits and vegetables. You can substitute a paring knife if you don't have a peeler.

Potato masher: This inexpensive utensil can mash potatoes and other vegetables.

Pots and pans: You'll need a small, medium, and large saucepan; a large skillet; and a stockpot, all with lids. I prefer stainless steel pots and pans. I also like to have one extra 12-inch nonstick frying pan to cook foods like eggs and French toast. A roasting pan is nice to have but not absolutely necessary; you may choose to purchase one when you think you can make frequent use of it.

Shop Right

There are lots of ways to make shopping as quick and enjoyable as possible. Here are some of my tips.

- **Make a list** of recipes you will be preparing for the week and make a shopping list from your recipes before heading to the grocery store. This will save you time and help you make sure that you get everything you need. Keep a running list of grocery needs during the week as well, and pick those things up during your weekly shopping trip.

- **Start your shopping** in the center of the grocery store and work your way to the outside areas. Most dry goods and pantry items are in the middle aisles of the store. The perimeter contains perishable items, such as meats; the produce and dairy sections; and the freezer aisles. Shopping these areas last will help keep your freezer and refrigerator items cold until you get home to unpack your groceries.

- **Take advantage** of the season and make recipes with whatever produce is abundant. This will allow you to get the freshest ingredients. The produce will last longer, and in-season produce is usually the tastiest and least expensive.

- **Buy groceries in bulk** if the items can be stored to stay fresh or if you have a large number of people to cook for. For example, if meat is on sale and you have freezer space, you can take advantage of the sale price. Just make sure the extra meat is double wrapped with plastic wrap and in plastic freezer bags when freezing. If you have neighbors to split costs with, go ahead and get the discounted bulk price and share with your friends.

- **Grocery shop during** off hours to save time. I never shop on the weekends unless it is absolutely necessary. To avoid the crowds, the best times to grocery shop are very early in the morning or after dinner.

Wire whisk: This utensil has wire loops and is used to whip, beat, or mix ingredients together.

Wooden and stainless steel spoons and spatulas: You should have a few spoons for mixing food. Wooden is essential for stirring hot ingredients, because a stainless steel spoon will conduct the heat to your hands. A metal spatula lifts foods like chicken, fish, or potatoes out of a pan. A rubber scraper spatula is useful to mix and scrape wet ingredients in a bowl.

ESSENTIAL APPLIANCES

Blender: This electric appliance blends together smoothies, sauces, and soups.

Electric hand mixer: This electric handheld appliance has rotating beaters that beat, whip, or mix ingredients together.

Microwave oven: Use it for melting butter and chocolate as well as reheating food.

Toaster: A simple countertop one is perfect for toasting bread.

NONESSENTIAL APPLIANCES

Immersion or stick blender: This inexpensive tool can purée sauces and soups right in the pot.

Slow cooker: It's nice to slow cook food while you are not home. You can put all the ingredients in it in the morning and come home to a cooked meal that evening.

Food processor: This appliance has interchangeable blades to chop, slice, dice, mince, shred, and purée.

Stock Your Pantry

My kitchen pantry is always stocked because I never know when I might need to cook a last-minute meal. Keeping the following essential ingredients in your kitchen will minimize your trips to the store. And who doesn't like to save time?

Also, the five main ingredients in every recipe in this book are not counting some of the basic pantry items listed here. I will give you the exact list in the next chapter.

PANTRY STAPLES

Black pepper: I use it to season many of my recipes. For a little more heat, I use red pepper flakes, too.

Canned tomatoes: These are the main ingredient in marinara sauce, and I often add them to soups and stews.

Storage Tips

- **Always keep your** refrigerator at 40°F or lower to avoid food spoilage. The freezer temperature should be kept at 0°F.

- **Do not overpack** your refrigerator or freezer, because air needs to circulate for your appliances to run properly. Overcrowding can cause temperatures to rise and food to spoil more quickly.

- **Keep any opened** packages of dry goods in airtight containers stored in a cool, dry place.

- **Never let cooked** foods sit out for more than 2 hours. Refrigerate or freeze leftovers as soon as possible. Make sure to label all freezer items with the contents and the date you froze them.

- **Check the "use by"** and "best by" dates on food products. Don't use a product after a "use by" date, as it may not be safe to eat. "Best by" dates are more flexible, as the product can still be used after the date expires, but the food may not be its best quality.

Cooking oils: Olive oil and canola oil are great for sautéing or panfrying, and I also use them in dressings.

Flour: White flour is a staple in baking and for thickening sauces.

Nonstick cooking spray: This is oil in a spray form, and it is perfect to use on a baking pan or nonstick pan to make sure food will not stick to the surface. If you do not have nonstick cooking spray, you can always brush some oil on a pan using a pastry brush or even a paper towel.

Pasta: We eat pasta at least once a week, and I love how shelf stable it is (meaning it can sit in your pantry for a while without spoiling).

Salt: Sea salt and kosher salt bring out the flavor in food. I use seasoned salt, too, because it adds a little more pizzazz than regular salt. Many of the recipes will call for salt or pepper "to taste" and not an exact amount.

Spices: Italian seasoning (a mixture of dried herbs), chili powder, garlic powder, cinnamon, and onion powder all add lots of flavor and are included in quite a few of the recipes in this book.

Sugar: Use white sugar for desserts and to add a bit of sweetness to sauces and dressings.

Vinegars: I love flavoring recipes with vinegar. It's low calorie and adds a perfect acid balance to food. My favorite types are balsamic, red wine, and cider vinegar.

FRESH STAPLES

Butter: This is a flavorful cooking fat for sautéing or baking. Unless a recipe specifically calls for salted butter, use unsalted butter so you can control the amount of salt in your meal.

Cream and milk: I use these often in my breakfast recipes, desserts, and creamy sauces.

Eggs: They're delicious for breakfast, but I also use them to bind together ingredients in many recipes.

Fresh herbs: Fresh herbs are used to brighten up flavors and garnish dishes.

Garlic: I occasionally use minced garlic from a jar for quick cooking, but if you are using it in salads or dressings, fresh garlic is always best.

Lemons: Lemon juice brightens up food. It's a great flavoring for seafood, desserts, and dressings.

You are now set with the basics for your kitchen. You have the right cooking tools, appliances, and staple ingredients, and your kitchen is well equipped to cook any recipe in this book.

Chapter 2

Get Cooking

YOUR KITCHEN IS PREPARED, but you're not going to start cooking just yet. First, I'll give you some tips on reading a recipe and getting ready to make it. Then, I'll go over basic knife and safety practices. I'll make sure you know the best way to measure ingredients and go over some basic cooking terms. After that, it's time to start trying out some of the recipes.

Be Prepared

One of the most important things you need to do before cooking is to read the recipe completely through. Since these recipes are short and simple, I have made this as painless as possible. Reading through the recipe will help you figure out what tools and ingredients you'll need and how much time you'll need for prep and cooking. It will help you avoid any mistakes or mis-understandings. Don't rush through the process, because it will pay off in the long run. Make sure you set aside enough time to make the recipe without taking any shortcuts.

Next, gather and measure your ingredients. It is also important to gather your cooking tools in advance. This makes everything less stressful when it's time to put together the ingredients.

Make sure to have a clean work space where you will be prepping everything. And prepare to clean up as you go along. Put dirty dishes and bowls right in the dishwasher so you don't have to worry about them later. I personally dislike cleaning up a big mess at the end of cooking, so I try to keep things as neat as possible. When I am done prepping and the food is cooking, I like to relax and take in the smell rather than having to do a lot of cleanup all at once. There is nothing like anticipating what you will be eating for dinner.

Turn on some music and make cooking fun! I love listening to my favorite tunes when I am preparing food. Make the process as enjoyable as possible.

Master the Knife

A few simple knife skills will go a long way when you're prepping food. If ingredients are cut properly, it is much easier to cook them. Food should be cut into uniform pieces so that it cooks evenly. Good cutting skills also make foods like salads look more attractive.

In the previous chapter, I recommended having a chef's knife and a paring knife. A paring knife is used to cut small pieces of food, like garlic, and to peel or trim fruits and vegetables. A chef's knife is essential and all-purpose. You can use it to cut practically everything.

To have good knife skills, the first thing you should do is get comfortable holding your chef's knife. There is really no one right way to hold a knife.

Safety First

Here are just a few safety tips I follow in my kitchen.

- **Wash your hands** before starting the cooking process and after handling meat or poultry.

- **Wear comfortable, fitted** clothing and never wear loose sleeves that could drag across the oven or stove and start a fire.

- **Keep long hair** tied back, both for fire safety and for sanitary purposes.

- **Keep all small** children and pets away from the hot stove or oven.

- **Use pot holders** to grab hot pots and pans from the oven or stove. Make sure handles are always turned in.

- **Never walk away** from an unattended pot or pan on the stove. It takes only seconds for a fire to start. In case of a grease fire, do not throw water on it. Sprinkling salt or baking soda on the fire is a good option to smother it if you do not have a fire extinguisher.

- **Separate raw meat,** poultry, and fish from other fresh foods to avoid cross-contamination of bacteria. Never let these perishable items sit out, because they can quickly spoil. They should be refrigerated or frozen right away.

- **Fruits and vegetables** should be washed before prepping, but do not wash meats, poultry, or fish, as this could spread bacteria. Cooking the food at proper temperatures should destroy all bad and dangerous bacteria.

- **Clean up all** spills promptly. Make sure the floor is dry so that no one slips and falls.

I prefer to "shake hands" with the handle of my knife. My index finger is on the outside of the blade and my other three fingers grip the top of the handle. Another way to hold a knife is to grip the handle as close to the blade as is comfortable, putting your thumb on the inside with your other fingers wrapped around the other side. The important thing is to hold the knife the way you feel most comfortable.

Always keep the top of the knife pointed down. The tip of the knife should not leave the cutting board. Cutting should be done using a rocking motion while you maneuver the handle up and down. The knife should be at the same height as your elbows, so you can use the weight of your upper body to put pressure on it. Make sure to cut away from your body so there are no accidents.

Your other hand will hold and guide the food on the cutting board. Make sure to curl your fingers and thumb inward a bit so that your knuckles act like a bumper or guide, keeping the tips of your fingers out of the way of the blade.

WHAT YOU DO WITH THE KNIFE

Now that you know some basics about holding and using a knife, here are the skills you will use to make the recipes in this book.

Chop: To cut food into small, uniform pieces. *Finely chopped* means smaller pieces, while *coarsely chopped* means larger, less pretty pieces.

Dice: To cut food into small cubes that are uniform in size. Typically, small dice is ⅛ inch wide, while large dice is ¾ inch wide.

Mince: To cut food into very small pieces. Usually food is minced so it can be dissolved when cooking. Garlic, herbs, and other aromatics are often minced.

Peel: To remove the skins off fruits and vegetables.

Slice: To cut long, thin pieces of food of similar thickness.

Trim: To cut off the ends or any part of the food that will not be eaten. For example, fat is trimmed off meat and stems are trimmed off strawberries.

Measure It Out

If you are new to cooking, measuring ingredients is a very important step in following a recipe. Eventually you will get to the point where you can eyeball some ingredients and not have to measure everything, but when you first start cooking, it's good to be precise. A set of measuring cups for dry ingredients, measuring spoons, and a transparent measuring cup for liquids are the perfect tools to keep your amounts exact.

To measure liquids, pour the ingredient directly into a transparent measuring cup set on a flat surface. Make sure you are looking at eye level when checking the measurement.

For dry ingredients, use plastic or metal measuring cups and spoons. Larger amounts of ingredients can be scooped up with the measuring cups, while smaller amounts will need measuring spoons. Flour is an exception: It should be lightly spooned into the measuring cup. Any extra on the top can be leveled off with a knife.

If you are measuring a semisolid ingredient, such as peanut butter or honey, you can also scoop it up with a measuring cup or spoon. Just make sure to use a rubber scraper to get every bit of the ingredient out of the cup or spoon.

Any time you see *packed* as part of a measurement (something like "¼ cup packed brown sugar") it means you fill the measuring cup or spoon to the top, and then push down the ingredient and add a bit more to bring the level back up to the top.

Cook It

It's important to know what the basic cooking technique terms mean so you can cook the way the recipe intends. Here are the techniques used in this book.

Bake: To cook with prolonged dry heat, typically in an oven. This is a very popular cooking method, as almost all food can be baked.

Baste: To pour cooking juices or fat over meat as it cooks to keep it moist and flavorful.

Broil: To cook under high direct heat. Food can be broiled in the last few minutes of cooking to either brown the top or quickly melt something gooey, such as cheese.

Brown: To partially cook the surface of meats or poultry to give it a golden brown color and crust.

Boil: To cook in a liquid that has reached 212°F and continuously has bubbles coming to the surface.

Braise: To cook first by browning, then over low heat in a small amount of liquid in a covered pan. Most stews are braised as this process gives food lots of flavor.

Caramelize: To brown the sugar in foods, resulting in a sweet, nutty flavor. Both fruits and vegetables will caramelize if cooked on high heat, due to their natural sugars.

Deglaze: To remove browned food residue from a pan by adding a bit of liquid and stirring and scraping everything into the liquid. This incorporates all the rich flavors into the sauce.

Grill: To apply dry heat directly to the surface of the food. It could be on an outside grill that has grates, or it could be on a very hot pan over the stove. This is a quick type of cooking and is healthier than frying because it uses very little fat.

Marinate: To soak food in a seasoned liquid (a marinade) that often includes an acidic element to tenderize the food or give it extra flavor.

Panfry: To cook food in a pan over medium-high heat in a small amount of fat. This is similar to sautéing, except the heat is a bit lower because you are cooking larger pieces of food for a longer time so it cooks all the way through. This is a healthy way of cooking because the food is not fully submerged in fat (which is called deep-frying).

Roast: To use dry high heat in a confined environment (your oven) so food forms a crust on the outside while it cooks all the way through.

Sauté: To cook food in a pan over relatively high heat with a small amount of fat. Sautéing is very similar to panfrying, except the heat is a bit higher because the pieces of food are smaller and cook quickly.

Sear: To cook food at an intense heat so that a crust is formed. Sometimes food is seared, then the heat is lowered so it cooks all the way through. Searing seals in flavor and the juices of meats, poultry, and seafood.

Simmer: To cook slowly over low heat just below the boiling point. You will see small bubbles when things simmer. Simmering is used frequently to cook sauces and soups.

About the Recipes

The great thing about this book is that the recipes are simple but not boring! Some are healthy, some are decadent, and some are my family's favorites. They all are convenient, delicious, and require only five main ingredients (plus your pantry staples). Here are the common staples that will not be counted as one of the five ingredients.

- Salt and seasoned salt

- Black pepper

- Water

- Vinegar

- Cooking oils

- Butter

- Nonstick cooking spray

- Common spices, such as garlic powder, cayenne pepper, chili powder, cinnamon, and Italian seasoning

Some recipes include optional ingredients or garnishes, which are clearly marked in case you would like to add them. A garnish is something that you sprinkle on top of a dish before serving; it's there more for visual appeal than for its flavor profile, which is why it's totally optional. When I have company over, I tend to add more garnishes to my food than when I am cooking a quick meal for my family.

When you see a seasoning, such as salt or black pepper, listed without an amount, that means you'll taste the dish and add as much as you want. And when you see the word *divided* after an ingredient, it means you'll use some of it in one step of the recipe and the rest in another step. Don't worry—I'll tell you exactly how much and when to add it in each step.

RECIPE LABELS

Included at the beginning of each recipe are special labels to describe the recipe's special features.

30-Minute: recipes that can be made in 30 minutes or less

Dairy-Free: for those of you avoiding dairy products

Freezer-Friendly: dishes that freeze well after being cooked

Gluten-Free: for those avoiding gluten, but there are dishes with oats included here, so be sure to get gluten-free oats if that's a concern for you

No-Cook: some prep, but no cooking at all

One Pot/Pan: only one pot or pan needed (less cleanup!)

Slow Cooker: made in a slow cooker, but I'll give you alternative instructions if you don't have one

Vegetarian: no meat or fish, but these dishes may have dairy or eggs

There is also an index in the back of this book where you can find the recipes organized under these labels. This is convenient when you need to look for a recipe in a specific category. My daughter follows a vegetarian diet, so I love being able to look at an index and see all the vegetarian options in one place.

TIPS

Every recipe in this book is followed by a tip. These tips will give you techniques or background information that will help you successfully cook all the recipes in this book. Here are the types of tips you'll find.

Prep Tip: how to get ingredients and tools ready to make preparation easier

Simple Swap: an ingredient substitution or different ways to prepare a recipe that can be equally tasty

Ingredient Tip: some information about an ingredient that may be unfamiliar to you

Leftovers: how the recipe can be easily stored for later use, or ways to revive or repurpose the meal

Technique Tutorial: an explanation of a cooking technique used in the recipe

Easy Variation: ways to make the recipe easier and/or faster to prepare

You now have all the ingredients, tools, equipment, and information you need to start cooking. It's time to make all the recipes in this book. Are you ready? I know you are!

Chapter 3

Breakfasts

Raspberry Lemon Yogurt Parfaits

Sweet raspberries pair well with tart lemon yogurt, and the creamy yogurt finds a contrast in the crunchy granola and almonds. You'll want this recipe in your weekly breakfast rotation, but it also works as a perfect snack.

Serves: 4
Prep time: 5 minutes

---

2 cups raspberries, plus
4 extra raspberries,
for garnish

4 (6-ounce) containers
lemon yogurt

½ cup granola

2 tablespoons sliced or
chopped almonds

1. Divide the raspberries evenly into four parfait glasses. Top each with half a container of yogurt.

2. Sprinkle each with granola. Top with the remaining yogurt. Sprinkle the almonds on top.

3. Garnish with the extra raspberries and serve.

Prep Tip: If you do not have parfait glasses, you can use cocktail or highball glasses. Small mason jars work too. It won't really matter what you put the parfaits in because as soon as you serve them, they will disappear.

Peanut Butter Banana Smoothies

30-MINUTE · GLUTEN-FREE · NO-COOK · VEGETARIAN

This smoothie is rich with protein and will give you lots of energy. It's the perfect morning pick-me-up. If you crave chocolate, you can make a chocolate peanut butter banana smoothie by adding ⅓ cup bottled chocolate syrup or Fuss-Free Chocolate Syrup (page 175) to the ingredients.

Serves: 4

Prep time: 5 minutes

4 small frozen ripe bananas, peeled and sliced

2 cups 2% milk

8 ounces vanilla Greek yogurt

¼ cup smooth peanut butter

1 cup ice

1. Add the bananas, milk, yogurt, peanut butter, and ice to a blender. Blend for 2 to 3 minutes, or until the mixture is smooth.

2. If you don't have a blender, put all the ingredients in a large bowl and beat on low with an electric hand mixer until all the lumps are gone. If the mixture is smooth but large pieces of ice remain, just pick them out with a spoon before transferring the smoothies to glasses.

3. Serve in tall glasses with straws.

Prep Tip: To store bananas in the freezer, peel and slice the bananas and seal each banana individually in a small freezer bag. Take them out when ready to use.

Smoked Salmon Bagel Bites

These delicious bagel bites are perfect for a quick breakfast but are also a great option if you are having company for brunch. They are easy to make but look like something served at a fancy tea party. I like them garnished with fresh chives, but feel free to substitute the same amount of fresh dill or parsley. Persian or baby cucumbers are smaller than regular cucumbers and are a great size for mini bagels. You can leave the skins on because they are thinner than the peel on a normal-size cucumber.

Serves: 4

Prep time: 10 minutes

8 mini bagels

8 ounces spreadable cream cheese

4 ounces thinly sliced smoked salmon

2 Persian or baby cucumbers, ends trimmed, thinly sliced

2 to 3 tablespoons chopped fresh chives

1. Cut the mini bagels in half horizontally. Spread a small amount of cream cheese on the cut side of each bagel half.

2. Top each bagel half with small pieces of smoked salmon and a few slices of cucumber. Sprinkle the chives on top.

Ingredient Tip: You can buy smoked salmon in vacuum-sealed packages in the seafood department of your grocery store. It is found next to the area that has prepackaged crab and other ready-to-eat seafood items.

Loaded Avocado Toast

Avocado toast is just slices of toasted bread with smashed avocado on them. This version gets loaded up with tomatoes, bacon, and cheese. Feel free to make it your own and add other toppings, such as fresh herbs, chopped onion, sliced ham, or diced peppers. Be sure to choose avocados with dark skin that yield a bit when you press them.

Serves: 6

Prep time: 15 minutes

6 slices whole-grain bread or another bread of your choosing

2 medium ripe avocados, peeled, pitted, and mashed

1 tablespoon olive oil

Pinch salt

2 medium plum tomatoes, chopped

6 slices bacon, cooked and crumbled

½ cup shredded Cheddar cheese

Black pepper

1. Lightly toast the bread in a toaster for 2 to 3 minutes.

2. In a medium bowl, combine the avocado, olive oil, and salt.

3. Spread the avocado mixture evenly on each slice of toast. Top evenly with tomatoes, bacon, and cheese.

4. Season with pepper to taste.

Prep Tip: To peel and pit an avocado, slice it horizontally with a sharp knife until you feel the knife hit the pit. Make sure you cut it all the way around. Twist the avocado to separate the halves. Remove the pit and scoop out the flesh with a spoon.

Perfect Scrambled Eggs

30-MINUTE · DAIRY-FREE · GLUTEN-FREE · ONE POT/PAN · VEGETARIAN

Every cook should know how to make these perfect scrambled eggs. Once you see how quick and easy this recipe is, scrambled eggs will be on your breakfast menu at least once a week. Pair them with some toast and fruit for a complete breakfast.

Serves: 4
Prep time: 5 minutes
Cook time: 5 minutes

---

8 large eggs

½ teaspoon salt, plus more for seasoning

2 tablespoons water

2 tablespoons salted butter

Black pepper

1. Crack the eggs into a medium bowl and whisk rapidly with salt and water for 30 seconds, or until the eggs are blended together and start to foam.

2. Melt the butter on low heat in a medium nonstick skillet. When the butter begins to bubble, add the egg mixture to the pan.

3. The eggs will start to cook in about 30 seconds. As they begin to get firm around the edges of the pan, use a heatproof rubber spatula to push them to the center of the pan. Stir as the eggs form large curds— soft but solid pieces of cooked egg within the liquid egg mixture. Remove the pan from the stove when all the eggs are firm but still soft and no visible liquid remains. This should be about 2 to 3 minutes of total cooking time.

4. Season with salt and pepper to taste.

Technique Tutorial: Whisking the eggs incorporates air into them, so the more muscle you use in whisking, the lighter and fluffier the eggs will be.

Spinach Feta Quiche

FREEZER-FRIENDLY · VEGETARIAN

Spinach Feta Quiche is a perfect breakfast dish but also versatile enough to make for a meatless lunch or dinner. This recipe uses premade refrigerated pie crust to make things easy. Purchase premade frozen pie crusts already in an aluminum pan and make this recipe even easier—just bring the crust to room temperature before you fill it. This quiche can be served warm or at room temperature.

Serves: 6
Prep time: 10 minutes
Cook time: 50 minutes

1 (10-ounce) package frozen spinach, defrosted and drained

1 cup whole milk

5 large eggs

6 ounces crumbled feta cheese with Mediterranean herbs (or plain)

1 refrigerated pie crust, brought to room temperature

1. Preheat the oven to 350°F.

2. Make sure all the water is drained and squeezed out of the spinach. You can use a colander for this.

3. In a medium bowl, mix together the spinach, milk, eggs, and cheese.

4. Unroll the pie crust and press it into a 9- to 10-inch pie plate. Crimp the edges with a fork (press the ends of the fork tines down on the rim, making sure to go around the whole rim) and make sure the pie crust is uniform all around the rim.

5. Pour the egg mixture into the pie crust, making sure not to overfill.

6. Bake for 45 to 50 minutes, or until the quiche is set and the crust is golden brown around the edges. A toothpick inserted in the center should come out clean.

7. Cool for 10 to 20 minutes before serving.

Simple Swap: If you prefer, use 10 ounces of fresh baby spinach in place of frozen spinach. Chop it up and sautée it in 1 tablespoon of olive oil in a large skillet over medium-high heat for a few minutes, or until it's wilted. The idea is to cook it until most of the water is removed. It can then be added to the egg mixture in step 3.

Broccoli and Ham Frittata Muffins

30-MINUTE · FREEZER-FRIENDLY · GLUTEN-FREE

These fluffy, handheld frittata muffins are easy to make and can be baked ahead of time. Just reheat them in the microwave. They are perfect for a weekday breakfast but also great to serve to a crowd at brunch.

Serves: 6
Prep time: 10 minutes
Cook time: 20 minutes

Nonstick cooking spray

1½ cups frozen chopped broccoli, defrosted

1 cup chopped deli ham

8 large eggs

½ cup 2% milk

1 teaspoon salt

¼ teaspoon black pepper

1 cup shredded Swiss cheese

1. Preheat the oven to 350°F.

2. Spray a nonstick 12-cup muffin tin liberally with nonstick cooking spray. Make sure all surfaces of the cups are coated.

3. In a medium bowl, mix together the broccoli and ham. Evenly divide the mixture between the 12 muffin cups.

4. In the same bowl, whisk together the eggs, milk, salt, and pepper. Mix in the cheese.

5. Pour the egg mixture over the broccoli and ham, making sure to divide it evenly among the 12 cups and filling almost to the top. Do not overfill; you don't want the egg mixture spilling over the side when baking.

6. Bake for about 20 minutes, or until the eggs are puffy and a toothpick inserted in the center of a frittata muffin comes out clean.

7. Let the pan cool for 5 to 10 minutes. Run a plastic knife around each cup to loosen the frittata muffins. Carefully remove with a rubber spatula.

Leftovers: Store leftovers in the refrigerator in an airtight plastic container. Frittata muffins can be reheated in the microwave for 30 to 60 seconds for a quick, easy breakfast. Frittata muffins can also be tightly wrapped individually with plastic wrap and stored in the freezer. Add about 30 seconds or more to the microwave time if they are coming from the freezer.

French Toast with Caramelized Bananas

French toast is the ultimate weekend breakfast, but this recipe is quick enough to enjoy on a weekday. If you love Bananas Foster, you'll love this French toast! Sprinkle on some chopped pecans or walnuts for an extra gourmet touch.

Serves: 4
Prep time: 10 minutes
Cook time: 15 minutes

---

3 eggs

¾ cup whole milk

8 slices brioche bread or potato bread

3 tablespoons butter (or more if needed), divided

¼ cup packed brown sugar

2 large bananas, peeled and sliced

1. In a medium shallow bowl, whisk together the eggs and milk.

2. Dip each piece of the bread in the egg mixture, then turn over, making sure both sides are soaked with the mixture.

3. Melt 2 tablespoons of butter in a large skillet over medium heat. When the butter has melted and is bubbling, add slices of the bread to the pan and cook about 2 minutes, or until golden brown. Flip the bread over and cook an additional 1 to 2 minutes, or until the other side is also golden brown. Repeat the process with the remaining bread, adding more butter if necessary.

4. As each piece is cooked, keep it warm on a plate covered with aluminum foil until the bananas are ready.

5. In a medium saucepan, melt the remaining 1 tablespoon of butter on medium-high heat. Add brown sugar and stir until the sugar dissolves. Add the bananas and stir to coat. Cook for 2 minutes or until the sauce starts to bubble.

6. Serve the French toast with the caramelized bananas on top.

Simple Swap: For an easy variation, make this with caramelized pears instead of bananas. Follow the recipe, but in step 5, melt 1 tablespoon of butter in a medium saucepan over medium-high heat. Add 3 ripe pears that have been peeled, cored, and sliced. Cook for 3 to 4 minutes, or until the pears are softened, then add ¼ cup packed brown sugar. Stir and cook until the sugar dissolves and the sauce is bubbling. Serve over the warm French toast.

Mexican Breakfast Burritos

30-MINUTE · ONE-POT/PAN · VEGETARIAN

These burritos are perfect for breakfast on the go. They are packed with protein and flavor, making them a great way to start the day. Make them in advance and they can be reheated in the microwave in just a minute or two.

Serves: 6
Prep time: 10 minutes
Cook time: 5 minutes

1 batch Perfect Scrambled Eggs (page 26)

1 cup canned black beans, rinsed

1 cup shredded Cheddar cheese

6 (10- to 12-inch) flour tortillas

¾ cup Three-Minute Blender Salsa (page 168) or your favorite jarred salsa, plus more for serving

Optional: Sour cream and guacamole for serving

1. Follow the recipe for Perfect Scrambled Eggs. Stir in the beans and cheese in the last 2 minutes of cooking.

2. Warm the tortillas in the microwave for about 10 seconds, so they are pliable.

3. Add some of the egg filling to the center of each tortilla. Top with a few spoonfuls of salsa. Wrap the burritos tightly.

4. Serve with sour cream and guacamole, if desired.

Technique Tutorial: To properly wrap a burrito, place the filling down the center of the tortilla in a horizontal line. Fold the side closest to you over the filling, then fold in the right and left sides so that none of the filling can fall out. Continue to tightly roll horizontally until all the filling is inside and the burrito is like a wrapped package.

Easy-as-Apple-Pie Oatmeal

30-MINUTE · GLUTEN-FREE · ONE POT/PAN · VEGETARIAN

If you like apple pie, you'll love a bowl of this warm oatmeal with apples, brown sugar, and walnuts. The sweet smell of cinnamon is a great way to start your morning. Whoever knew something so delicious could also be so heart-healthy?

Serves: 4
Prep time: 10 minutes
Cook time: 15 minutes

---

2 medium apples, peeled

1 tablespoon butter

¼ cup packed light brown sugar

4 cups water

2 cups old-fashioned rolled oats

½ teaspoon salt

½ tablespoon cinnamon

½ cup chopped walnuts

Optional: Milk, for serving

1. Cut the peeled apples in quarters and use a paring knife to cut out the core and seeds. Coarsely chop the apples into pieces.

2. In a large saucepan, melt the butter on medium heat. Add the apples and cook for 5 minutes, or until they begin to soften. Stir in the brown sugar.

3. Pour the water into the pan and bring the mixture to a boil. Add the oats, salt, and cinnamon. Turn heat to low and cook for 5 minutes, or until the oats are fully cooked and the oatmeal is creamy.

4. Serve the oatmeal in bowls sprinkled with walnuts. Stir in milk, if desired.

Leftovers: For a quick, easy breakfast, make this recipe in advance and store the oatmeal in an airtight plastic container in the refrigerator. Reheat in a microwave-safe bowl for about 90 seconds in the microwave, or until the oatmeal is steaming hot.

Chapter 4

Snacks

Chocolate-Cranberry Trail Mix

30-MINUTE · DAIRY-FREE · GLUTEN-FREE · NO-COOK · VEGETARIAN

This may be the easiest recipe you will ever make. Five ingredients are mixed together to create your own trail mix. Why buy a packaged mix when you can make your own?

Serves: 6
Prep time: 5 minutes

½ cup shelled salted almonds

½ cup sweetened dried cranberries

¼ cup semisweet chocolate chips

¼ cup shelled sunflower seeds

¼ cup shelled salted roasted peanuts

1. Mix all ingredients together in a medium bowl.

2. Store in an airtight container until you are ready to eat.

Leftovers: Double or triple the recipe so that you have snacks for weeks or months. As long as you store this in an airtight container in a cool place, it will keep for 6 months.

Frozen Chocolate-Covered Bananas

This fun treat is easy to put together and will make any summer day delicious. I like to keep these in my freezer all year round for a nice guilt-free snack. If you don't like coconut, substitute ½ cup of your favorite type of chopped nuts instead.

Serves: 6

Prep time: 20 minutes, plus 2 hours to freeze

1 (12-ounce) bag semisweet chocolate chips

2 tablespoons coconut oil (or canola oil)

3 bananas, peeled and halved crosswise

6 Popsicle sticks or wooden skewers

½ cup sweetened shredded coconut

1. In a shallow microwavable bowl, mix together the chocolate chips and coconut oil. Microwave until the chips are fully melted.

2. Line a rimmed baking sheet with parchment paper. Insert a Popsicle stick or skewer in the cut end of each banana. Dip the banana halves in the melted chocolate until they are fully covered. Sprinkle with the shredded coconut and place on the lined baking sheet.

3. Freeze on the baking sheet until the chocolate is set and the bananas are frozen, about 2 hours. Transfer to an airtight container or freezer bag and keep in the freezer until ready to serve.

Technique Tutorial: To melt chocolate, microwave on medium (or use the chocolate setting, if you have one) for 60 seconds. Stir, and then continue to microwave on medium and stir every 30 seconds until there are just a few lumps of chocolate left. Remove from the microwave and stir until all the chocolate is melted.

Maple Cinnamon Roasted Almonds

GLUTEN-FREE · VEGETARIAN

These nuts are just like the ones you get hot at a festival or carnival, but with a little less sugar, making them a healthier snack. It's best to use raw, unsalted almonds—find them in the baking or bulk section—since you'll be roasting and adding salt yourself.

Serves: 6
Prep time: 5 minutes
Cook time: 10 minutes

---

2 cups raw
unsalted almonds

1 tablespoon salted
butter, melted

2 tablespoons pure
maple syrup

1 tablespoon brown sugar

½ teaspoon cinnamon

¼ teaspoon salt

1 tablespoon white sugar

1. Preheat the oven to 325°F. Line a rimmed baking sheet with parchment paper.

2. In a medium bowl, mix together the almonds, butter, maple syrup, and brown sugar. Stir until the almonds are fully coated.

3. Spread the almonds on the baking sheet in a single layer. Bake for 10 to 15 minutes. Check on them every 5 minutes to give them a stir and make sure they don't burn.

4. While the almonds are baking, mix together the cinnamon, salt, and white sugar in the same bowl you used to mix the almonds.

5. Remove the almonds from the baking sheet, place in the bowl with the cinnamon and sugar mixture, and toss to coat.

6. Cool for a few minutes before serving. Store any leftovers in an airtight container.

Technique Tutorial: When a recipe calls for melted butter, you can melt it in the microwave. Place the butter in a small microwavable bowl and cover with a paper towel so that it can't splatter. Heat the butter on low in 20-second increments until melted. You can also melt it in a small pan on the stove using very low heat.

Raspberry Ricotta Toast

My kids are not sure if Raspberry Ricotta Toast is a snack, a breakfast, or a dessert. I say it's all three! For a delicious variation, you can substitute a cup of blueberries or sliced strawberries for the raspberries.

Serves: 4
Prep time: 5 minutes
Cook time: 5 minutes

4 slices bread

1 cup raspberries

2 tablespoons honey

½ cup whole milk or part-skim ricotta cheese

1. Lightly toast the bread in a toaster for 2 to 3 minutes.

2. In a small bowl, mix together the raspberries and honey.

3. Spread an equal amount of ricotta cheese on each slice of toasted bread. Top each slice with one quarter of the raspberry mixture.

Easy Variation: You can substitute frozen raspberries if fresh are not available. Just be sure to defrost the berries overnight in a bowl covered with plastic wrap in the refrigerator. Drain them in a colander before using.

Lemon Rosemary Spiced Olives

DAIRY-FREE · GLUTEN-FREE · VEGETARIAN

There's no need to buy fancy olives from a specialty store when you can make them at home using a can of plain, inexpensive olives. I always keep some of these olives in the refrigerator to serve with cheese if unexpected guests stop by. Not only are they delicious, but spicing these up yourself saves you money.

Serves: 6
Prep time: 5 minutes, plus 8 hours to chill
Cook time: 5 minutes

¼ cup olive oil

2 garlic cloves, chopped

Juice of 1 small lemon

2 teaspoons dried rosemary

1 (6-ounce) can green olives, drained

1. Heat the oil in a small saucepan over low heat. Add the garlic to the pan and cook for a few minutes until fragrant. Do not let the garlic turn brown. Stir in the lemon juice and rosemary.

2. Put the olives in an airtight container. Pour the olive oil mixture over the olives, and mix well. Keep the olives stored in the refrigerator for at least 8 hours before serving.

Simple Swap: You can substitute red wine vinegar for lemon juice if you'd like to give the olives a bit of a different flavor.

Cheesy Black Bean Nachos

30-MINUTE · GLUTEN-FREE · ONE-POT/PAN · VEGETARIAN

Get ready for game day with these cheesy nachos! They are easy to make and can be served right from the baking sheet. My kids love them so much that sometimes I add 1½ cups of shredded cooked chicken before I add the cheese, and we call it dinner.

Serves: 4
Prep time: 10 minutes
Cook time: 5 minutes

6 ounces corn tortilla chips (half a 13-ounce bag)

1 (15-ounce) can black beans, rinsed and drained

1 teaspoon chili powder

2 cups shredded Cheddar cheese

Three-Minute Blender Salsa (page 168)

Optional: Sour cream and guacamole for serving

1. Preheat the oven to 400°F. Line a rimmed baking sheet with foil or parchment paper.

2. Arrange the chips in a single layer on the lined baking sheet.

3. In a small bowl, mix the beans with the chili powder. Spoon them over the tortilla chips. Sprinkle with the cheese.

4. Bake for 6 to 8 minutes or until the cheese is melted and gooey. Top with as much salsa as you like. Serve with sour cream and/or guacamole, if desired.

Prep Tip: Line your baking sheet with a precut sheet of parchment paper. I buy these already-cut sheets in a box. It makes cleanup so easy!

Pepperoni Pizza Dip

GLUTEN-FREE · ONE-POT/PAN

Pizza seems to be everyone's favorite food, so I decided to make it into a dip. You can serve it with crackers, breadsticks, or slices of bread, but corn tortilla chips or veggie sticks (like celery and carrots) are great options, too, if you want to stay gluten-free.

Serves: 6
Prep time: 10 minutes
Cook time: 25 minutes

8 ounces cream cheese, softened

1½ teaspoons dried Italian seasoning, divided

2 cups shredded mozzarella cheese, divided

1 cup Basic Marinara Sauce (page 173) or your favorite jarred sauce

¼ cup grated Parmesan cheese

⅓ cup mini pepperoni slices, or larger slices cut into smaller pieces

1. Preheat the oven to 350°F.

2. In a medium bowl, mix together the cream cheese, 1 teaspoon of Italian seasoning, and 1 cup of mozzarella cheese.

3. Spread the mixture in a 2-quart casserole dish or 9-inch pie pan. Top with the marinara sauce.

4. Sprinkle the remaining 1 cup of mozzarella cheese and the Parmesan cheese on top, followed by the remaining ½ teaspoon of Italian seasoning. Top with the pepperoni slices.

5. Bake for 20 to 25 minutes or until the cheese is bubbly and golden.

6. Serve with whatever you want to dip into it.

Technique Tutorial: To shred mozzarella cheese, use the side of a box grater with the largest holes for a coarse texture. To grate Parmesan cheese, use the side with the smallest holes, which will give the cheese a fine texture.

Simple Cheddar Biscuits

30-MINUTE · ONE-POT/PAN · VEGETARIAN

My kids love coming home from school to the smell of fresh-baked Cheddar biscuits. They are the perfect afternoon snack. I also like using them as a base for breakfast sandwiches. Scallions are a wonderful addition to make these biscuits a little more special. I make them this way and pair them with soup or chili.

Serves: 6
Prep time: 10 minutes
Cook time: 15 minutes

1 cup all-purpose flour

2 teaspoons baking powder

¼ cup salted butter, melted

½ cup buttermilk

½ cup shredded Cheddar cheese

Optional: 2 to 3 tablespoons chopped scallions

1. Preheat the oven to 425°F. Line a rimmed baking sheet with parchment paper.

2. In a medium bowl, whisk together the flour and baking powder. Stir in the butter and buttermilk. Mix gently until combined, making sure not to overmix. The batter should be blended but also have some lumps in it.

3. Fold in the cheese and the scallions, if using.

4. Drop 6 mounds of dough (about ⅓ cup each) onto the baking sheet. Bake for 8 to 11 minutes, or until the edges of the biscuits start to turn golden brown. If you would like bigger biscuits, make 4 mounds of dough instead of 6. The recipe will then make 4 biscuits. An extra few minutes of baking time might be needed.

Simple Swap: If you do not have buttermilk, add ½ tablespoon of lemon juice or white vinegar to a liquid measuring cup. Fill to the ½-cup line with whole milk. Let the mixture sit for 10 minutes before using. This is a perfect substitute for buttermilk.

Chapter 5

Salads and Sandwiches

Mediterranean Spinach Salad

30-MINUTE · GLUTEN-FREE · NO-COOK · VEGETARIAN

This salad is healthy, quick, and easy to make. I love it for lunch, but it is also on my family's dinner menu quite often. To make it a main dish salad, add 8 ounces of chopped cooked chicken before tossing with the dressing.

Serves: 6
Prep time: 10 minutes

10 to 12 ounces
baby spinach

1 cup canned chickpeas,
rinsed and drained

½ cup crumbled
feta cheese

2 cups grape tomatoes

⅓ cup Simple Italian
Vinaigrette (page 166)
or your favorite bottled
vinaigrette

1. In a large bowl, mix together the spinach, chickpeas, cheese, and tomatoes.

2. Toss the salad with the dressing right before serving.

Prep Tip: Baby spinach is sold in 6-ounce bags and 10-ounce bags. Use either two smaller bags or one larger bag. You can usually find bags of prewashed spinach that is ready to add to your salad.

Italian Wedge Salad

30-MINUTE · GLUTEN-FREE · NO-COOK · VEGETARIAN

An Italian salad with simple vinaigrette has always been one of my favorites. I love the wedge presentation, but you could chop up all the ingredients and toss it with dressing if you'd prefer a chopped salad instead. Either way, it's delicious!

Serves: 4
Prep time: 10 minutes

½ head iceberg lettuce

1 cup grape tomatoes, halved

6 ounces diced salami

6 ounces diced provolone cheese

⅓ cup Simple Italian Vinaigrette (page 166) or your favorite bottled vinaigrette

Optional: ½ cup sliced black olives

1. Cut the lettuce into 4 equal wedges. Place them on individual plates or on a large platter.

2. Top each lettuce wedge with evenly divided amounts of the tomatoes, salami, and cheese. Drizzle the dressing on the salads.

3. Top with black olives, if desired.

Prep Tip: Buy the salami and provolone cheese from the deli section at your grocery store. You can get it thickly sliced, then just dice it up before tossing it in the salad.

Tomato and White Bean Salad

30-MINUTE · GLUTEN-FREE · NO-COOK · ONE POT/PAN · VEGETARIAN

This salad is super easy to make, and it's a great side dish to complement chicken, fish, beef, or pork. It's a good choice to bring to potluck or picnic dinners, too. Double the recipe and you will have plenty to feed a crowd.

Serves: 6
Prep time: 10 minutes

1 (15-ounce) can white beans, rinsed and drained

1 pint grape tomatoes, halved

3 tablespoons chopped fresh basil

⅓ cup crumbled feta cheese

¼ cup Simple Italian Vinaigrette (page 166) or your favorite bottled vinaigrette

Black pepper

1. In a medium bowl, mix together the beans, tomatoes, basil, and cheese.

2. Drizzle the dressing over the salad and mix well.

3. Add pepper to taste.

Leftovers: Store leftovers overnight in an airtight container in the refrigerator. This salad is great served on a bed of greens for lunch the next day.

Spicy Cucumber Salad

30-MINUTE · DAIRY-FREE · GLUTEN-FREE · NO-COOK · VEGETARIAN

This Spicy Cucumber Salad doesn't include mayonnaise or sour cream, as some cucumber salads do. This makes it perfect for outdoor picnics and barbecues. I was introduced to a similar cucumber salad when I visited a Korean restaurant, and I decided to recreate the dish. I like my cucumber salad spicy, but you can add as much or as little red pepper as you want.

Serves: 4

Prep time: 10 minutes

2 tablespoons rice vinegar

1 teaspoon sea salt, plus more if needed

1 tablespoon sugar

1 tablespoon sesame oil

1 large English cucumber, ends trimmed, thinly sliced

Pinch red pepper flakes

1. In a medium bowl, whisk together the rice vinegar, salt, sugar, and sesame oil until the sugar dissolves.

2. Add the cucumber slices and red pepper to the bowl. Mix well and season with more salt, if desired.

3. The salad can be made in advance and refrigerated before serving.

Ingredient Tip: English cucumbers are large, seedless cucumbers found in the produce section of the grocery store. You can substitute 3 smaller pickling (kirby) cucumbers, if you can't find English cucumbers.

Strawberry Blue Cheese Arugula Salad

30-MINUTE · GLUTEN-FREE · NO-COOK · VEGETARIAN

This fresh salad is the perfect combination of savory, sweet, and salty. It works well as a side dish with dinner but also makes a perfect lunch all on its own. In just 10 minutes, you can have this gorgeous salad on your table.

Serves: 4
Prep time: 10 minutes

3 tablespoons olive oil

2 tablespoons balsamic vinegar

1 tablespoon honey

6 ounces arugula

2 cups sliced strawberries

⅓ cup crumbled blue cheese

Salt

Black pepper

1. In a small bowl, whisk together the oil, vinegar, and honey for about 30 seconds, or until well blended. Set aside.

2. Put the arugula in a large bowl. Top with the strawberries. Add the dressing and toss well, so all the greens and strawberries are coated. You can use more or less dressing, depending on your taste.

3. Sprinkle the cheese on top.

4. Season with salt and pepper to taste.

Simple Swap: For a tangy variation, use feta or goat cheese instead of the blue cheese.

Cucumber Hummus Wraps

30-MINUTE · NO-COOK · VEGETARIAN

I love rolling up hummus and vegetables in a flatbread or tortilla to make a quick lunch. The great thing about this wrap is that you can add additional ingredients, such as thinly sliced tomatoes, roasted peppers, or spinach. You'll never get tired of packing this in your lunch box.

Serves: 4
Prep time: 10 minutes

½ cup hummus

4 thin flatbread wraps or large tortillas

1 small cucumber, ends trimmed, thinly sliced

⅓ cup chopped olives

¼ cup crumbled feta cheese with Mediterranean herbs

Optional: roasted red peppers, baby spinach, thinly sliced tomatoes

1. Spread the hummus on one side of each flatbread or tortilla.

2. Top each with equally divided amounts of cucumbers, olives, and cheese.

3. Add any optional ingredients desired before rolling.

4. Roll each flatbread or tortilla tightly, making sure to tuck in the sides.

Leftovers Prep Tip: These wraps are perfect to make for lunch the night before because the flavors will blend together better. Make the wraps, then tightly wrap in foil. Your lunch is now ready for the next day.

Bacon and Avocado Grilled Cheese

30-MINUTE · ONE POT/PAN

Bacon and avocado make this grilled cheese sandwich over-the-top. Mayonnaise is spread on the outside and inside of the bread to give the sandwich a creaminess and golden-brown crust. You'll never go back to plain grilled cheese again!

Serves: 4
Prep time: 10 minutes
Cook time: 20 minutes

4 tablespoons mayonnaise

8 slices whole-grain bread

8 thick slices Cheddar cheese

8 slices cooked bacon, warmed in the microwave

1 large avocado, peeled, pitted, and cut into 12 slices

1. Spread mayonnaise on both sides of each slice of bread.

2. On 4 of the slices of bread, layer 1 slice of cheese, 2 slices of bacon, 3 slices of avocado, and another slice of cheese. Top with the remaining cheese and bread slices.

3. Heat a large nonstick skillet or griddle over medium heat. Place the sandwiches in the skillet. Cook for 4 to 5 minutes on each side, or until the bread is golden brown and the cheese is melted. If all the sandwiches can't fit into the skillet at once, cook in two batches.

4. Cut the sandwiches in half before serving.

Prep Tip: Precooked bacon is sold in packages at your grocery store. For easy prep, the slices can be heated in the microwave oven on a plate, between two paper towels, for 15 to 20 seconds.

Easy Cuban Turkey Sammies

I grew up in an area with great little Cuban restaurants that had the best sandwiches. This is my version of a grilled Cuban sandwich, using deli turkey instead of the traditional roasted pork. Instead of the pickles and mustard most Cuban sandwiches are made with, I use mustard relish, since it contains both ingredients. If you prefer, or can't find mustard relish, you can substitute 4 tablespoons of mustard and 2 large sliced dill pickles. Either way, these sandwiches will be delicious!

Serves: 4
Prep time: 10 minutes
Cook time: 10 minutes

4 tablespoons butter

8 slices sourdough bread or white bread

6 tablespoons mustard relish

8 slices Swiss cheese

8 slices roasted deli turkey

4 slices smoked deli ham

1. Butter one side of each slice of bread and spread mustard relish on the other side of each slice.

2. Heat a large nonstick pan over medium heat. Place four slices of bread in the pan with the buttered side down. Top each with 1 slice of cheese, 2 slices of turkey, 1 slice of ham, and some pickle slices. Top with another slice of cheese and another slice of bread with the buttered side up.

3. Cook for 2 to 4 minutes on each side, or until sandwiches are golden brown and the cheese is melted. If all the sandwiches can't fit into the skillet at once, cook in two batches. Keep the first sandwiches warm on a plate loosely covered with foil.

Simple Swap: If you would like a more traditional Cuban sandwich, swap 8 slices of roasted pork for the deli turkey. You can buy it at the deli counter of your grocery store.

Pizza Quesadillas

30-MINUTE · ONE POT/PAN · VEGETARIAN

My kids love quesadillas, and they love pizza just as much. One evening when they were having a hard time deciding which they wanted, I decided to combine both. Once you try these, you won't go back to making plain cheese quesadillas anymore. Pepperoni makes these quesadillas even more delicious.

Serves: 4
Prep time: 10 minutes
Cook time: 15 minutes

---

4 large flour tortillas

½ cup Basic Marinara Sauce (page 173), plus more for dipping

1 cup shredded mozzarella cheese

1 teaspoon dried basil

1 tablespoon olive oil, plus more if needed

Optional: 16 small slices pepperoni

1. Lay the tortillas on a cutting board and spread an equal amount of marinara sauce over half of each tortilla. Top the sauce with an equally divided amount of cheese and sprinkle with basil. Add 4 pieces of pepperoni to each quesadilla, if using.

2. Fold each quesadilla in half, folding the plain half of the tortilla over the side with toppings.

3. Heat the olive oil in a large nonstick skillet over medium heat. Cook two quesadillas at a time for about 2 to 3 minutes, until golden brown on one side. Flip over and continue to cook on the second side until the cheese is melted and the tortilla is golden brown, about 2 minutes more. Repeat with the two remaining quesadillas, adding more olive oil if needed.

4. Remove from the pan and cut each quesadilla into wedges. Serve with additional marinara sauce for dipping, if desired.

Easy Variation: Instead of making your own marinara sauce, use your favorite brand of jarred pizza sauce.

Caprese Ham Panini

30-MINUTE · ONE POT/PAN

You don't need a panini press to make these delicious grilled sandwiches. In the summer, I love using fresh tomatoes and basil from my garden. To make this sandwich vegetarian, omit the ham and add a few extra slices of tomato.

Serves: 4
Prep time: 10 minutes
Cook time: 15 minutes

---

1 tablespoon olive oil, plus more if needed

4 tablespoons butter, softened

4 square ciabatta rolls or round Italian rolls, split in half horizontally

8 slices (about 12 ounces) fresh mozzarella cheese

8 slices deli ham

12 fresh basil leaves, chopped

2 large plum tomatoes, thinly sliced

1. Heat a large skillet over medium heat. Coat the pan with the olive oil.

2. Spread butter on the cut side of each roll. Put 4 halves of the rolls in the pan, cut side up. If your pan fits only 2 halves of the rolls, cook them in two batches, adding more olive oil if needed.

3. Lay equally divided amounts of cheese and ham on all pieces of the bread in the pan. Cover the pan with a lid to keep the heat in, and cook for 3 to 4 minutes, or until the cheese is melted.

4. Lay the basil and tomatoes over the ham.

5. Cover the sandwiches with the remaining pieces of bread.

6. Turn the sandwiches over and press them while cooking for 3 to 4 minutes, or until the bread turns golden brown. Remove the sandwiches from the pan and cut in half before serving.

Technique Tutorial: To press sandwiches, put a lid on top of the sandwiches that is smaller than the diameter of your pan. Press down on the lid so the sandwiches flatten a little. Keep the lid on top of the sandwiches until the sandwiches are golden brown and the cheese is melted.

Chapter 6

Soups and Stews

Creamy Tomato Basil Soup

30-MINUTE · FREEZER-FRIENDLY · GLUTEN-FREE · ONE POT/PAN · VEGETARIAN

This creamy tomato soup is pure comfort food. It is perfect with a grilled cheese sandwich. I also frequently eat this as a light lunch, paired with a crusty piece of bread for dipping.

Serves: 4
Prep time: 10 minutes
Cook time: 20 minutes

---

1 (32-ounce) carton vegetable broth

2 (14.5-ounce) cans fire-roasted diced tomatoes

2 garlic cloves, minced

½ tablespoon dried basil

½ cup heavy cream

Salt

Black pepper

2 tablespoons finely chopped fresh basil

1. Combine the broth, tomatoes, garlic, and dried basil in a medium saucepan over medium heat. Cook for 5 minutes, or until the mixture comes to a low boil.

2. When the soup starts to bubble, reduce the heat to low and stir in the heavy cream.

3. Simmer for 15 minutes, stirring occasionally. Remove the pot from the heat and use an immersion blender to purée the soup. If you do not have an immersion blender, you can pour the soup into a regular blender and purée for 30 seconds, or until it's smooth.

4. Season with salt and pepper to taste.

5. Serve the soup in four bowls and top each bowl with the chopped fresh basil.

Simple Swap: If you cannot find fire-roasted tomatoes, use regular diced tomatoes and add 2 teaspoons of chili powder to the soup to give it a slightly smoky flavor.

Potato Soup

30-MINUTE · FREEZER-FRIENDLY · GLUTEN-FREE · ONE POT/PAN · SLOW COOKER

This is a simple, creamy potato soup that is plenty tasty on its own but can also be topped with extras, such as shredded cheese, bacon, or diced ham. A fun idea is to serve a potato soup bar for dinner. Serve up the soup and have a variety of toppings ready for everyone to add to their bowl.

Serves: 6
Prep time: 10 minutes
Cook time: 30 minutes

5 medium russet potatoes

2 tablespoons butter

1 medium yellow onion, peeled and diced

1 (32-ounce) carton low-sodium chicken broth

½ cup heavy cream

Salt

Black pepper

Optional: crumbled bacon, shredded Cheddar cheese, diced ham, chopped chives, chopped scallions, chopped parsley

1. Peel and dice the potatoes into small cubes, about ¾ inch. You should end up with about 6 cups of potatoes.

2. Melt the butter in a large pot over medium heat. Sauté the onions for 5 minutes, or until soft. Add the chicken broth and potatoes to the pot. Turn the heat to medium-high and bring to a boil.

3. Reduce the heat to low, cover, and cook for 20 minutes, or until the potatoes are soft. Add the cream.

4. Blend the soup with an immersion blender until creamy. Add a little water to thin it out, if necessary. If you don't have an immersion blender, blend in a blender for about 30 seconds or until creamy, then pour the soup back into the pot.

5. Season with salt and pepper to taste.

6. Serve in bowls, garnished with whatever extra toppings you choose.

Leftovers: This soup can be frozen without the toppings in airtight containers. Defrost the soup in the refrigerator overnight and then reheat in a medium pot on the stove for 10 to 15 minutes, or until the soup comes to a simmer. Add a little milk if the mixture gets too thick. Add the toppings at the end, after you reheat the soup.

Pastina Egg-Drop Soup with Spinach

30-MINUTE · ONE POT/PAN

My Italian grandmother frequently made stracciatella. The name might be a little hard to say, but it's really just a cheese and egg drop soup. Spinach and pastina (tiny bits of pasta) are added to this one, making it extra delicious. To make this soup vegetarian, just substitute vegetable broth for the chicken broth.

Serves: 6
Prep time: 10 minutes
Cook time: 15 minutes

---

8 cups low-sodium chicken broth

6 ounces fresh baby spinach, chopped

1½ cups dried pastina pasta

3 large eggs, beaten

¼ cup grated Parmesan cheese, plus more for serving

Salt

Black pepper

1. In a large saucepan or soup pot, bring the broth to a boil over medium-high heat. Add the spinach and pastina. Reduce the heat to medium. Cook the pasta for about 8 minutes, or until tender.

2. In a bowl, mix together the eggs and grated cheese. Add the egg mixture to the soup and stir well.

3. Season with salt and pepper to taste. Serve with extra grated Parmesan cheese.

Technique Tutorial: To add the egg mixture to the soup, slowly drizzle the mixture into the hot broth. With your other hand, stir the soup gently as you are pouring in the egg mixture. Remove the pot from the heat and let the soup stand for about 30 seconds to finish cooking the eggs.

Chicken Orzo Soup

DAIRY-FREE · ONE POT/PAN

They say chicken soup is good for the soul, and I believe that. I make this go-to soup whenever a family member or friend is feeling under the weather. There's no need to spend all day in the kitchen when you can make this quick version instead.

Serves: 4
Prep time: 10 minutes
Cook Time: 30 minutes

---

1 tablespoon olive oil

1 small onion, peeled and finely chopped

2 medium carrots, peeled and chopped

1 (32 ounce) carton low-sodium chicken broth

1 large (6-ounce) boneless, skinless chicken breast

½ cup dried orzo

Salt

Black pepper

Optional: 2 tablespoons chopped fresh parsley

1. In a large saucepan, heat the olive oil over medium heat. Add the onion and carrots. Sauté for 3 minutes, or until the veggies start to soften.

2. Pour in the broth and add the chicken breast to the saucepan.

3. Bring the broth to a boil and then reduce heat to low. Simmer the chicken breast for 15 minutes, or until it is no longer pink and is cooked through. Remove the chicken breast and cool on a cutting board.

4. Stir the orzo into the broth and cook for 7 to 10 minutes, or until tender. Chop up the chicken breast and put it back in the pot of soup.

5. Season with salt and pepper to taste. Stir in the parsley, if using.

Ingredient Tip: Use low-sodium chicken broth so you can control the amount of salt in the soup. You can always add more salt, but once it's in, you can't take it out.

Easy Beef Veggie Soup

FREEZER-FRIENDLY · GLUTEN-FREE · ONE POT/PAN

This very hearty soup is freezer-friendly, so you can make it in advance for a nourishing meal on a cold night. There have been so many times when I've come home from a busy day and was happy to remember that I had this easy meal in the freezer. This soup is very good food!

Serves: 6
Prep time: 10 minutes
Cook time: 90 minutes

---

2 tablespoons olive oil

1 pound beef top round cubes

6 cups low-sodium beef broth

1 (14-ounce) can diced tomatoes with onions and garlic

4 small potatoes, peeled and chopped

1 (12-ounce) bag frozen mixed vegetables

Salt

Black pepper

1. In a large saucepan or soup pot, heat the olive oil over medium-high heat for 1 or 2 minutes, then add the meat. Cook for about 5 minutes, or until the meat starts to brown.

2. Add the broth and tomatoes. Bring to a boil, turn the heat to low, cover with a lid, and simmer for 60 minutes. If too much broth evaporates, you can add a little water.

3. Add the potatoes and vegetables. Cook for another 15 to 20 minutes, or until the potatoes are tender. Season with salt and pepper to taste.

Leftovers: Make a double batch of this in a stockpot and store the leftovers in small individual airtight containers in the freezer. It makes the perfect lunch to reheat in the microwave.

Tortellini and Smoked Sausage Soup

30-MINUTE · ONE POT/PAN

This hearty and comforting soup has been on my dinner menu for years. It is a complete meal that includes pasta, meat, and vegetables. This is a great way to get a meal on your table in under half an hour.

Serves: 6
Prep time: 10 minutes
Cook time: 20 minutes

8 cups low-sodium chicken broth

12 ounces smoked sausage, cut into ¼ inch thick pieces

1 medium yellow onion, peeled and chopped

2 large carrots, trimmed, peeled, and coarsely chopped

2 (9-ounce) packages frozen cheese tortellini

Salt

Black pepper

1. In a large saucepan over high heat, add the chicken broth, smoked sausage, onion, and carrots. Bring to a boil, reduce the heat to medium, and cook for 10 minutes.

2. Add the frozen tortellini and cook for about 5 minutes more, until tender, or according to the package instructions.

3. Season with salt and pepper to taste before serving.

Simple Swap: You can use another kind of tortellini, such as spinach, meat, or pesto. The grocery store has so many great kinds to choose from.

Sausage, Beans, and Greens Soup

FREEZER-FRIENDLY · DAIRY-FREE · GLUTEN-FREE · ONE POT/PAN

I love the combination of sausage, beans, and greens. To make this soup healthier, substitute lean turkey or chicken sausage for the pork sausage. You can't go wrong with any of them. Bulk sausage is the sausage meat without the casing. If you can't find it anywhere, buy sausages with the casing, slit the casing open with a paring knife, and peel it back to remove the sausage meat.

Serves: 6
Prep time: 10 minutes
Cook time: 35 minutes

1 tablespoon olive oil

1 pound bulk Italian pork sausage

6 cups low-sodium chicken broth

1 large head kale, stemmed and coarsely chopped

3 large potatoes, peeled and chopped

1 (15-ounce) can white beans, rinsed and drained

1 tablespoon dried Italian seasoning

Optional: red pepper flakes

1. In a large soup pot, heat the olive oil over medium-high heat for 1 to 2 minutes. Add the sausage and cook for about 10 minutes, or until it is no longer pink. Stir, using a wooden spoon, to break the sausage up into pieces. Drain the sausage in a colander to remove any grease. Place the sausage back in the pot.

2. Add the broth, kale, and potatoes. Cook for 15 minutes, or until the potatoes are tender.

3. Add the beans and Italian seasoning. Mix well and cook for 10 minutes more. If the soup is too thick, add a little water to thin it out. Season with red pepper flakes, if desired.

Prep Tip: The easiest way to prep kale for recipes is to do it when you first bring it home from the grocery store. Remove the thick center stalk and chop the leaves in small pieces. Rinse and drain them in a colander. Dry the kale with paper towels and store in resealable plastic bags or an airtight plastic container. I like to place a few paper towels in between the layers of greens to absorb any extra moisture. Use within a few days.

White Bean and Corn Chili

30-MINUTE · DAIRY-FREE · FREEZER-FRIENDLY · GLUTEN-FREE
ONE POT/PAN · SLOW COOKER · VEGETARIAN

When I want vegetarian comfort food, this chili is what I make. It's really freezer-friendly so I always keep a batch frozen to reheat for a quick and easy dinner. It's also easy to make in the slow cooker, too, so if you have one, you can let your appliance do all the work. Just put all the ingredients in your slow cooker (defrost the corn first) and mix it well. Cook on low for 6 hours or on high for 4 hours. Make sure to add a little water if it gets too thick.

Serves: 6
Prep time: 5 minutes
Cook time: 25 minutes

1 tablespoon olive oil

1 medium yellow onion, peeled and diced

1 to 2 tablespoons chili powder (depending how much spice you like)

2 (14-ounce) cans diced tomatoes with green chilies

1 (10-ounce) package frozen corn

2 (15-ounce) cans white beans, rinsed and drained

Salt

Black pepper

Optional: shredded Cheddar cheese, sour cream, chopped fresh cilantro

1. In a large pot, heat the olive oil over medium-high heat for 1 to 2 minutes. Add the onion and sauté for about 5 minutes, or until soft.

2. Add the chili powder, tomatoes, and corn. Cook for a few minutes until the chili comes to a boil. Add the beans.

3. Reduce the heat to low and bring the chili to a simmer. Cover with a lid and cook for 15 minutes. If the chili gets too thick, add a few tablespoons of water. Season with salt and pepper to taste.

4. Serve the chili with your favorite optional toppings.

Leftovers: Freeze the chili in an airtight container. To reheat, let it defrost in your fridge overnight, then put it in a medium pot and heat on the stove over medium heat for 15 minutes, or until the chili is simmering. Add a little water if it gets too thick.

Slow Cooker Hunter-Style Chicken Stew

DAIRY-FREE · FREEZER-FRIENDLY · GLUTEN-FREE · ONE POT/PAN · SLOW COOKER

My mother and grandmother would often make a big pot of chicken in a red sauce for our Sunday dinner. This stew is similar, and can be served with pasta or rice. I like to soak up the sauce and vegetables with a nice crusty loaf of bread. Use gluten-free bread if that's a concern for you.

Serves: 6
Prep time: 10 minutes
Cook time: 4 to 8 hours

2 medium onions, peeled and chopped

1 (14-ounce) can diced tomatoes with onion and garlic

2 carrots, peeled and chopped

1 tablespoon dried Italian seasoning

6 large pieces skinless chicken (legs or thighs)

1 teaspoon seasoned salt, plus more to taste

½ teaspoon black pepper

1 pound mushrooms, sliced

1. In a 6-quart slow cooker, mix together the onions, tomatoes, carrots, and Italian seasoning. Add the chicken on top and sprinkle with the seasoned salt and pepper. Scatter the mushrooms on top and cover.

2. Cook on low for 6 to 8 hours or high for 4 to 6 hours, or until the chicken is tender but hasn't fallen off the bone.

3. Stir well when the chicken is cooked, and serve the sauce and vegetables over the chicken.

Easy Variation: If you do not have a slow cooker, you can make this on the stove. In a large pot over medium heat, add the onions, tomatoes, carrots, and Italian seasoning. Bring to a simmer and add the chicken, seasoned salt, pepper, and mushrooms. Stir well and bring to a boil. Reduce the heat to low, cover, and simmer for about 40 minutes, or until the chicken is fork-tender. Add water ½ cup at a time if the sauce gets too thick. Keep the heat low and add water as necessary so the chicken and sauce don't stick to the pan.

Slow Cooker Red Wine and Beef Stew

DAIRY-FREE · FREEZER-FRIENDLY · SLOW COOKER

Everyone should know how to make a good beef stew. This one is easy and can be served with mashed potatoes, pasta, or rice. If you don't have a slow cooker, you can use the Easy Variation to cook it on your stove.

Serves: 6
Prep time: 10 minutes
Cook time: 4 to 6 hours

1½ pounds cubed beef

2 teaspoons seasoned salt, plus more if needed

½ teaspoon black pepper

2 tablespoons all-purpose flour

1 tablespoon olive oil

1 cup red wine

2 medium onions, peeled and cut into quarters

4 large carrots, peeled and cut into 2-inch pieces

1. Put the beef pieces in a large bowl and sprinkle with the seasoned salt and pepper. Then add the flour and toss to coat.

2. In a large skillet, heat the olive oil on medium for 1 minute and cook the meat for about 10 minutes, or until it is browned. Add the wine to the pan to deglaze. Transfer the meat and juices to a heated slow cooker.

3. Stir in the onions and top with the carrots.

4. Cook for about 6 hours on low or 4 hours on high. The meat and vegetables should be fork-tender when done. Season with more seasoned salt, if desired.

Easy Variation: If you do not have a slow cooker, you can make this stew in a large soup pot. Follow step 1. Then, instead of using a skillet, brown the meat in the oil over medium heat right in the pot. Add the wine, onions, carrots, and 1 cup of water. Bring to a boil, then turn the heat to low and cover. Simmer for 1½ to 2 hours, or until the meat is fork-tender. Add extra water as needed if the liquid evaporates too quickly.

Chapter 7

Vegetables and Sides

Buttery Corn on the Cob

30-MINUTE · GLUTEN-FREE · ONE POT/PAN · VEGETARIAN

Summer barbecues demand corn on the cob. This is a great make-ahead side dish to serve to a crowd. You add a little milk to the pot to make the corn extra sweet and tender.

Serves: 6
Prep time: 15 minutes
Cook time: 15 minutes

---

6 large ears of corn, shucked

1 cup whole milk

3 tablespoons butter, melted

Salt

Black pepper

1. Fill a large pot halfway with water. Bring to a boil over medium-high heat.

2. Add the corn (the cobs can be cut in half, if you want) and milk. Turn the heat to medium and cook the corn for 6 to 10 minutes, depending how tender you like it, with a few more minutes if you like it more tender.

3. Turn the heat off, but you can keep the corn warm in the pot for up to an hour until you're ready to serve it.

4. Remove the corn from the water and drizzle the butter over it. Season with salt and pepper to taste.

Technique Tutorial: Here is the easiest way to shuck corn. Cut off the stalk end of each cob right above the first row of kernels with a sharp knife. Place 3 ears of corn on a microwave-safe plate. Microwave on full power for about 60 seconds. Hold the corn by the uncut end in one hand while shaking the ear up and down until the cob slips free, leaving the husk and silk behind. Repeat with the other 3 ears of corn.

Simply Roasted Asparagus

30-MINUTE · DAIRY-FREE · GLUTEN-FREE · ONE POT/PAN · VEGETARIAN

I could eat asparagus at dinner every night. It's a delicious vegetable and also one of the easiest to prepare. Turn your oven on and you will have this delicious vegetable ready in 20 minutes.

Serves: 6
Prep time: 5 minutes
Cook time: 20 minutes

2 pounds
asparagus, trimmed

2 tablespoons olive oil

1 teaspoon garlic powder

½ teaspoon salt

¼ teaspoon black pepper

1. Preheat the oven to 400°F.

2. In a large bowl, toss the asparagus with olive oil and sprinkle with the garlic powder, salt, and pepper, making sure to coat well. Place on a large rimmed baking sheet.

3. Roast for about 15 minutes, or until the asparagus is as tender as you like it.

Ingredient Tip: Pick bunches of asparagus that have a rich green color and purple highlights with a small amount of white on the bottom. The stalks should be firm and the tips should not be mushy. To trim the asparagus, just snap off the bottoms as the perfect amount of the stalk will snap right off. It is best not to store asparagus for more than a few days and to cook it as soon as possible.

Honey Glazed Carrots

30-MINUTE · GLUTEN-FREE · ONE POT/PAN · VEGETARIAN

These carrots are what I call "vegetable candy." Serve them with poultry, fish, or meat and they will brighten up any dinner. All it takes is a little butter and honey to turn these into mouthwatering gems. Carrots are typically sold in 1-pound bags, so no need to weigh what you buy for this recipe.

Serves: 6
Prep time: 5 minutes
Cook time: 25 minutes

---

1 pound carrots, peeled

½ teaspoon salt

2 teaspoons dried parsley

2 tablespoons butter, melted

2 tablespoons honey

1. Preheat the oven to 425°F. Line a rimmed baking sheet with parchment paper.

2. Cut the carrots into 2-inch-thick rounds.

3. In a medium bowl, toss them with the salt, parsley, butter, and honey until evenly coated. Spread the carrots on the baking sheet.

4. Bake for 20 to 25 minutes, or until the carrots are tender.

Easy Variation: Substitute a 1-pound bag of baby carrots for regular carrots. Then you can skip the peeling and cutting.

Honey Balsamic Roasted Brussels Sprouts

30-MINUTE · DAIRY-FREE · GLUTEN-FREE · ONE POT/PAN · VEGETARIAN

These are on my dinner menu often. Roasting Brussels sprouts brings out their nutty flavor, and the balsamic vinegar and honey bring out their sweetness. If you never thought you could love a Brussels sprout, this recipe will change your mind.

Serves: 4
Prep time: 10 minutes
Cook time: 20 minutes

---

1 pound Brussels sprouts, trimmed and halved

2 tablespoons olive oil

¾ teaspoon sea salt

¼ teaspoon black pepper

1 teaspoon garlic powder

2 tablespoons balsamic vinegar

2 tablespoons honey

1. Preheat the oven to 400°F. Line a rimmed baking sheet with parchment paper.

2. In a large bowl, toss the Brussels sprouts with the olive oil, salt, pepper, and garlic powder.

3. Place the Brussels sprouts on the baking sheet and roast them for 20 minutes, or until they are tender and starting to brown on the outside.

4. While they are cooking, mix the balsamic vinegar and honey in a small bowl and stir until the honey is dissolved.

5. Place the roasted Brussels sprouts back in the large bowl. Add the vinegar and honey mixture. Toss them until they are evenly coated before serving.

Easy Variation: To make this recipe even easier, buy Brussels sprouts already cleaned in a 1-pound bag. All you'll have to do is cut them in half.

Roasted Broccoli with Lemon, Garlic, and Parmesan

GLUTEN-FREE · ONE POT/PAN · VEGETARIAN

Roasted broccoli is healthy and is a perfect complement to chicken, meat, or fish. The garlic, lemon juice, and Parmesan cheese give this side dish lots of flavor. And the leftovers are great in a salad for lunch the next day.

Serves: 6
Prep time: 10 minutes
Cook time: 30 minutes

2 medium heads broccoli, trimmed and cut into florets

2 tablespoons olive oil

1 tablespoon crushed or minced garlic

½ teaspoon kosher salt

¼ teaspoon black pepper

1 teaspoon freshly squeezed lemon juice

¼ cup grated Parmesan cheese

1. Preheat the oven to 400°F.

2. Cut the broccoli florets into bite-size pieces. Place the broccoli in a large bowl and toss with the olive oil, garlic, salt, and pepper, making sure to coat well.

3. Spread the broccoli out on a large rimmed baking sheet and place in the oven. Roast for 25 to 30 minutes, until the broccoli is tender and starts to look crispy.

4. Toss the roasted broccoli with the lemon juice and cheese before serving.

Prep Tip: To cut the broccoli into florets, first remove the tough fibrous bottom of the stalk by cutting it off. Trim off any small branches using a paring knife. Peel off the tough outer layer of the stem. Separate the stem and the florets. You can save the stem for soup or another use. Trim the florets so they can be cut into smaller pieces.

Cinnamon Roasted Butternut Squash

DAIRY-FREE · GLUTEN-FREE · ONE POT/PAN · VEGETARIAN

Roasting brings out the sweetness of butternut squash. Whenever I make this recipe, I realize I don't cook butternut squash often enough. Not only is it a healthy vegetable, but your house will smell delicious every time you roast it with cinnamon.

Serves: 4
Prep time: 10 minutes
Cook time: 30 minutes

---

1 medium butternut squash (about 2 pounds), peeled, seeded, and cut into cubes

1 tablespoon olive oil

2 tablespoons light brown sugar

1 teaspoon kosher salt

½ teaspoon ground cinnamon

¼ teaspoon black pepper

1. Preheat the oven to 400°F. Line a rimmed baking sheet with parchment paper.

2. Place the squash cubes in a large bowl. Toss with the olive oil, brown sugar, salt, cinnamon, and pepper. Make sure the squash is coated evenly.

3. Place the squash on the baking sheet in one layer.

4. Roast for 15 minutes, turn the cubes with a spatula, then return to the oven and cook for another 10 to 15 minutes, or until the squash is tender and the outsides have started to brown.

Prep Tip: To prepare your butternut squash for roasting, microwave it whole for 30 seconds to make the skin easier to remove, then cut off the ends. You can now stabilize the squash because it has a flat end. Next, peel it with a peeler. It's easiest to do it lengthwise in long strokes. Once it's peeled, cut the squash in half lengthwise and scoop out the seeds. The halves can now be cut into slices, then into cubes. Or you can buy precut butternut squash to make prep even easier. It's sold in bags or plastic containers in the produce section of your grocery store.

Sweet and Spicy Pickled Vegetables

DAIRY-FREE · GLUTEN-FREE · ONE POT/PAN · VEGETARIAN

As a child, I would help my mother and grandmother make refrigerator pickles out of cucumbers from the garden. But why not use all sorts of vegetables? I use carrots, cauliflower, and jalapeño peppers in this recipe, but feel free to try some onions or red bell peppers, too.

Serves: 6
Prep time: 10 minutes, plus 1 hour to marinate
Cook time: 10 minutes, plus overnight to pickle

3 large carrots, peeled and cut into 1-inch rounds

2 cups cauliflower florets

2 jalapeño peppers, seeded and thinly sliced

1½ tablespoons sea salt

1½ cups white vinegar

¾ cup sugar

1 tablespoon pickling spices

½ cup water

1. Place the carrots, cauliflower florets, and jalapeños in a large bowl. Sprinkle with the salt and toss well. Let the mixture sit for 1 hour.

2. In a small saucepan, mix together the vinegar, sugar, pickling spices, and water. Place over medium-high heat and bring to a boil. Stir until the sugar is dissolved. Remove from the heat.

3. Place the vegetables in glass or plastic containers and pour the vinegar mixture over them.

4. Let the vegetables sit in the fridge for 24 hours before serving.

Leftovers: Pickled vegetables can be stored in an airtight glass jar or plastic container in the refrigerator for up to 30 days.

Saucy Tomato Green Beans

DAIRY-FREE · GLUTEN-FREE · ONE POT/PAN · VEGETARIAN

I have a friend who cooks great Greek food, and I always look forward to eating the green beans she makes. This recipe was inspired by those beans that I love to eat at her house. These braised green beans take some extra time to cook, but once they are on the stove, the work is minimal.

Serves: 6
Prep time: 15 minutes
Cook time: 45 minutes

2 tablespoons olive oil

2 garlic cloves, minced

1 (14-ounce) can diced tomatoes with basil and garlic

2 teaspoons dried Italian seasoning

1 teaspoon salt

½ teaspoon black pepper

1 tablespoon sugar

1 cup water

1 pound green beans, trimmed

1. Heat the olive oil over medium heat in a large saucepan. Sauté the garlic for 2 minutes, or until fragrant.

2. Add the tomatoes, Italian seasoning, salt, pepper, sugar, and water to the pan. Bring the mixture to a boil and stir in the green beans. Toss the beans in the sauce to coat.

3. Cover and cook on low heat for 20 minutes. Remove the lid and cook for another 20 minutes, or until the beans are tender to your taste and half the liquid is evaporated.

Prep Tip: Trimming green beans can be a tedious chore. To make it as easy as possible, line up the beans in several bunches on a cutting board. Trim off the tips on one end, then do the other side. Repeat with the next batch until they are all trimmed.

Sautéed Blue Cheese Mushrooms

30-MINUTE · ONE POT/PAN · VEGETARIAN

These creamy mushrooms are perfect with steak or pasta. I also like them on slices of toasted Italian bread. Not only are the mushrooms delicious, but you will want to make sure you get every bit of sauce that goes with them.

Serves: 6
Prep time: 5 minutes
Cook time: 10 minutes

2 tablespoons olive oil

1 pound white mushrooms, sliced

¼ cup heavy cream

2 tablespoons chopped fresh parsley

¼ cup crumbled blue cheese

Salt

Black pepper

1. In a large skillet or frying pan, heat the olive oil over medium heat. Add the mushrooms and cook for about 8 minutes, or until tender.

2. Add the heavy cream and parsley. Stir and cook for another 3 minutes, or until the sauce is simmering and blended together. Stir in the blue cheese.

3. Season with salt and pepper to taste.

Simple Swap: Parmesan cheese can easily be substituted for the blue cheese. Just add ¼ cup of grated Parmesan when the cream is added. If the sauce gets too thick, adding a few spoonfuls of cream will thin it out.

Zucchini Au Gratin

I frequently serve this zucchini as a side dish, however, my vegetarian daughter eats it as a main course. I make a side of rice or pasta to go with it, and it makes a really delicious meal!

Serves: 4 to 6
Prep time: 10 minutes
Cook time: 35 minutes

2 tablespoons olive oil

2 garlic cloves, minced

3 medium to large zucchini, cut into ¼-inch rounds

1 teaspoon salt

¼ teaspoon black pepper

½ cup tomato sauce

¼ cup grated Parmesan cheese

¼ cup panko breadcrumbs

1. Preheat the oven to 350°F.

2. Heat the olive oil in a large skillet over medium heat. Add the garlic and zucchini. Cook for 5 minutes, or until the zucchini starts to soften. Sprinkle on the salt and pepper. Stir in the tomato sauce and cook for 5 more minutes, or until the sauce starts bubbling.

3. Transfer the mixture to a medium baking dish or a 9-inch pie pan. Sprinkle the cheese and breadcrumbs on top.

4. Bake for 20 to 25 minutes, or until the casserole is bubbling. Turn the oven to broil for the last 2 minutes so the top gets golden brown. Cool for at least 5 minutes before serving.

Simple Swap: Substitute yellow summer squash for the zucchini. This dish is good with either, or you could use a combination of the two.

Roasted Eggplant Veggie Medley

DAIRY-FREE · GLUTEN-FREE · ONE POT/PAN · VEGETARIAN

I make a big batch of roasted vegetables almost every week, and this is one of the recipes I use. These vegetables make their own sauce, so they are great to spoon over chicken, fish, or pasta. They are healthy but delicious and a great way to get everyone to eat their vegetables.

Serves: 6
Prep time: 10 minutes
Cook time: 35 minutes

1 medium eggplant, peeled and cubed into bite-size pieces

10 ounces mushrooms, sliced

1 red bell pepper, seeded and cut into ½-inch strips

3 plum tomatoes, coarsely chopped

1 medium onion, peeled and coarsely chopped

1 tablespoon dried Italian seasoning

1 teaspoon salt, plus more if needed

¼ teaspoon black pepper, plus more if needed

1 teaspoon garlic powder

2 tablespoons olive oil

1. Preheat the oven to 400°F. Line a large rimmed baking sheet with parchment paper.

2. In a large bowl, mix the eggplant, mushrooms, bell pepper, tomatoes, and onion. Sprinkle on the Italian seasoning, salt, pepper, and garlic powder. Toss with the olive oil to coat well.

3. Spread out the mixture on the baking sheet and roast for 25 to 35 minutes, or until the vegetables are tender to your liking.

Leftovers: I love to make a double batch of these vegetables. They are great reheated in the microwave and perfect to serve in tortilla wraps, mixed in with scrambled eggs, or tossed with pasta.

Herb-Roasted Red Potatoes

DAIRY-FREE · GLUTEN-FREE · ONE POT/PAN · VEGETARIAN

Roasted potatoes are a staple in my house and make a perfect side dish to so many dinners. No need to peel the potatoes because the skin contains most of the vitamins, and these red potato skins are very thin. I like to switch up the herbs I use. This dish is also wonderful with parsley in place of the rosemary, or you can try making it with several different types of herbs.

Serves: 6
Prep time: 5 minutes
Cook time: 35 minutes

2 pounds baby red potatoes, scrubbed, dried with paper towels, and halved

2 tablespoons olive oil

1 teaspoon salt

½ teaspoon black pepper

2 teaspoons dried Italian seasoning

2 teaspoons garlic powder

1 to 2 tablespoons chopped fresh rosemary (depending on your taste)

1. Preheat the oven to 400°F. Line a large rimmed baking sheet with parchment paper.

2. In a large bowl, toss the potatoes with the olive oil, salt, pepper, Italian seasoning, garlic powder, and rosemary, making sure they are evenly coated.

3. Spread the potatoes on the baking sheet and roast about 20 minutes, turn them with a spatula, and roast 15 minutes more. The potatoes will be done when they are fork-tender and crispy golden on the outside.

Simple Swap: You can swap baby Yukon Gold potatoes for red potatoes, or you can use regular-size potatoes. Just cut them into quarters.

Creamy Sour Cream Mashed Potatoes

30-MINUTE · FREEZER-FRIENDLY · ONE POT/PAN · VEGETARIAN

Mashed potatoes are the ultimate comfort food! They can be served alongside fish, poultry, or meat. My family loves them topped with my 10-Minute Gravy (page 172). But they're great with no gravy at all, too.

Serves: 6
Prep time: 5 minutes
Cook time: 25 minutes

---

3 pounds yellow potatoes, peeled and cut into 2-inch cubes

3 tablespoons butter, plus more if desired

¾ cup milk

¾ cup sour cream

1 teaspoon salt

¼ teaspoon black pepper

1. Place the potatoes in a large pot of water on medium-high heat. Bring to a boil and reduce the heat to low. Cover and simmer the potatoes for 15 to 20 minutes or until they are tender. Drain the potatoes in a colander and return them to the pot.

2. Add the butter, milk, sour cream, salt, and pepper to the potatoes. Mash them with a potato masher until smooth. Add a little more milk, if necessary.

3. Serve topped with an additional pat of butter, if desired.

Technique Tutorial: To mash potatoes, use a masher in an up-and-down motion and keep mashing until you get the desired consistency. Use a wooden spoon to blend them together after they have been mashed. If you would like extra-creamy potatoes, you can mash the potatoes, then beat them with a hand beater for about 60 seconds or until they are the smoother texture you desire.

30-Minute Potato Hash

30-MINUTE · DAIRY-FREE · GLUTEN-FREE · ONE POT/PAN · VEGETARIAN

These potatoes are versatile enough to serve with dinner or for breakfast. My family loves them for brunch with some scrambled eggs on top. Stir in some precooked crumbled bacon toward the end of the cooking time for extra flavor!

Serves: 4
Prep time: 10 minutes
Cook time: 20 minutes

---

4 medium baking potatoes

1 tablespoon olive oil

2 tablespoons salted butter

1 medium yellow onion, peeled and finely chopped

1 cup diced red bell peppers

½ teaspoon salt

¼ teaspoon black pepper

1. Microwave the potatoes for 5 to 7 minutes or until soft. Dice them into bite-size pieces.

2. In a large nonstick pan or skillet, heat the olive oil and butter over medium-high heat. Add the onions and bell peppers. Cook for about 5 minutes, or until the vegetables start to soften, stirring often.

3. Add the potatoes to the veggies, reduce the heat to medium, and cook for about 10 minutes, or until the potatoes are tender and start to turn golden brown. Season with the salt and pepper before serving.

Technique Tutorial: To microwave potatoes, pierce them with a fork a few times, put them in a microwavable bowl, and cover the bowl with a paper towel. Cook on high until the potatoes are softened, 5 to 7 minutes. Let them cool for a few minutes, then you can slip off the skins (or leave them on, depending on your preference) before dicing.

Maple Mashed Sweet Potatoes with Pecans

This recipe is always a favorite on my Thanksgiving table, but I don't just make it on holidays. These sweet potatoes are a perfect side dish for chicken, turkey, or any meat. My personal preference is serving them with pork.

Serves: 6
Prep time: 10 minutes
Cook time: 20 minutes

2 pounds sweet potatoes, peeled and cut into 2-inch cubes

¼ cup light cream

2 tablespoons salted butter

½ teaspoon salt

2 tablespoons pure maple syrup

¼ cup finely chopped toasted pecans

1. Place the sweet potatoes in a large pot of water over medium-high heat. Bring to a boil and reduce the heat to low. Simmer the potatoes for 15 to 20 minutes, or until they are tender. Drain the potatoes in a colander and return them to the pot.

2. Add the cream, butter, and salt to the sweet potatoes and mash until smooth. Mix in the maple syrup. If you like your sweet potatoes extra creamy, beat them with a hand beater for about 60 seconds or until smooth.

3. Sprinkle the pecans over them right before serving.

Prep Tip: You can make these mashed sweet potatoes ahead of time and then reheat them in your oven. This can be especially helpful for holiday dinners. Make the sweet potatoes without the pecans and store in the refrigerator in a covered casserole dish. To reheat, mix in a few spoonfuls of light cream, cover, and place in a preheated 350°F oven for about 30 minutes, or until heated through. Stir a few times in the middle of the baking time. Sprinkle with pecans before serving.

Easy Tangy Cole Slaw

30-MINUTE · DAIRY-FREE · GLUTEN-FREE · ONE-POT/PAN · VEGETARIAN

This cole slaw is perfect to make for a picnic since it contains no mayonnaise, so there are no worries about keeping it out too long when it's hot out. My family loves it with pulled pork or chicken sandwiches, and I also use it as a taco topping. It has a little bit of sweetness and a whole lot of tangy goodness. I never have an outdoor gathering without making this cole slaw!

Serves: 4

Prep time: 20 Minutes

¼ cup cider vinegar

3 tablespoons sugar

1 teaspoon seasoned salt

2 tablespoons canola or vegetable oil

1 (16-ounce) bag shredded cabbage and carrot mix

2 tablespoons chopped fresh parsley

Salt

Black pepper

1. In a small sauce pan, mix together the vinegar, sugar, seasoned salt, and oil. Turn on the stove to medium heat and cook for 5 to 10 minutes or until mixture comes to a boil. Stir the mixture until the sugar is dissolved then remove from the heat.

2. In a large bowl, toss the bagged cabbage with the dressing and parsley. Mix well. Season with salt and pepper to taste.

3. Let the mixture stand for 10 minutes before serving or refrigerate and serve at a later time.

Leftovers Tip: This slaw is great for entertaining because it can be made the night before, if desired. Sometimes it will draw extra liquid from sitting in the refrigerator so just make sure to drain it well if you prepare it in advance. The recipe can be doubled for serving a crowd.

Chapter 8

Pasta and Grains

Baked Ziti Marinara

FREEZER-FRIENDLY · VEGETARIAN

Baked ziti was something I grew up on. It was served at many family dinners, including holidays. I frequently make this for dinner, as it is the ultimate comfort food.

Serves: 6
Prep time: 10 minutes
Cook time: 30 minutes

Nonstick cooking spray

12 ounces uncooked ziti

3 cups Basic Marinara Sauce (page 173), or store-bought sauce

1 cup ricotta cheese

2 cups shredded mozzarella cheese, divided

½ cup grated Parmesan cheese

1. Preheat the oven to 350°F. Spray a 3-quart casserole dish with nonstick cooking spray.

2. In a large pot of water over high heat, boil the ziti for about 8 minutes, until al dente (or according to the package directions). Drain and add the ziti back to the pot. Turn off the heat.

3. Mix in the marinara sauce, then stir in the ricotta cheese, 1 cup of mozzarella cheese, and the Parmesan cheese.

4. Put the pasta mixture into the casserole dish and sprinkle with the remaining 1 cup of mozzarella cheese. Loosely cover with foil.

5. Bake for 20 minutes. Remove the foil and bake another 10 minutes, until cheese is bubbly and starts to brown.

Prep Tip: This is a freezer-friendly meal that can be made ahead of time in a disposable foil pan. Follow the instructions up to step 4, then double wrap the whole thing tightly in aluminum foil and plastic wrap before storing it in the freezer. When you are ready to bake it, remove the plastic wrap and loosen the foil. Bake it in a preheated 350°F oven for 50 to 60 minutes, or until the cheese is bubbling and the casserole is heated through.

Easy-as-the-Box Mac and Cheese

30-MINUTE · ONE POT/PAN · VEGETARIAN

Macaroni and cheese is my son's favorite, and I have always kept a few boxes in our pantry. But once I made this recipe, a box could not be found in my kitchen again. It's so easy that now my son makes it for the whole family.

Serves: 6
Prep time: 5 minutes
Cook time: 15 minutes

1 pound uncooked elbow macaroni

3 tablespoons butter

3 tablespoons all purpose flour

3½ cups whole milk

1 teaspoon salt

12 ounces sharp Cheddar cheese, shredded (about 3 cups)

½ cup grated Parmesan cheese

1. In a large pot of water over high heat, boil the macaroni for 6 to 8 minutes, until al dente (or according to the package directions). Drain well.

2. In the same pot, melt the butter on medium heat and stir in the flour to form a paste. Mix with a wire whisk and slowly add the milk, whisking all the time. Stir in the salt. Cook on low heat for 3 to 5 minutes, whisking often, until the sauce is thickened. It should start to bubble when it thickens.

3. Add the cheeses and mix well until the sauce is smooth.

4. Stir in the cooked macaroni and mix well, until the pasta and sauce are well combined. Cook for another 1 to 2 minutes, or until the sauce is the desired thickness. Serve warm.

Simple Swap: Switch the Cheddar and Parmesan cheeses for 3½ cups of shredded pepper jack cheese to give the dish some spiciness.

Creamy Pesto Gnocchi

30-MINUTE · ONE POT/PAN · VEGETARIAN

Gnocchi are great to keep in the pantry for a quick meal. These little pillows of deliciousness are made from flour and potatoes, and take under 15 minutes to cook. The decadent pesto cream sauce will entice you to make this for dinner once a week.

Serves: 4
Prep time: 5 minutes
Cook time: 15 minutes

---

1 (16- to 18-ounce) package gnocchi

1 tablespoon butter

¼ cup store-bought pesto

¼ cup heavy cream

Salt

Black pepper

2 tablespoons chopped fresh basil

Optional: grated Parmesan cheese

1. In a large pot of water over high heat, boil the gnocchi for 2 to 4 minutes, until tender (or according to the package directions). Drain, reserving ½ cup of the pasta water.

2. Heat the butter over medium heat in a large skillet. Add the pesto, cream, and reserved pasta water. Stir in the gnocchi and gently mix together.

3. Reduce the heat to low and cook for 2 to 3 minutes, or until the sauce is creamy, stirring occasionally. Season with salt and pepper to taste.

4. Sprinkle with the basil and serve with Parmesan cheese, if desired.

Simple Swap: For an equally tasty dish, substitute 1 pound of cheese tortellini for the gnocchi.

Fettuccine Parmesan Pasta

30-MINUTE · VEGETARIAN

Fettuccine Alfredo is the ultimate comfort food that you can find on every Italian restaurant menu. This creamy dish is very similar and can be made in under 30 minutes. I add some fresh parsley to make this pasta dish as fresh and colorful as possible.

Serves: 6
Prep time: 5 minutes
Cook time: 25 minutes

1 pound uncooked fettuccine

3 tablespoons salted butter

2 garlic cloves, minced

1 cup half-and-half

½ cup grated Parmesan cheese

Salt

Black pepper

Chopped fresh parsley, for garnish

1. In a large pot of water over high heat, boil the fettuccine for about 12 minutes, until al dente (or according to the package directions). Drain, reserving ½ cup water from the pasta.

2. Melt the butter over medium heat in a large frying pan. Add the garlic and cook for 3 to 4 minutes, until it starts to turn fragrant.

3. Add the half-and-half and Parmesan cheese to the pan. Whisk for about 30 seconds or until smooth, and cook for a few minutes or until the sauce starts to thicken.

4. Add the cooked fettuccine to the pan, along with the reserved pasta water. Toss with the sauce until the pasta is well coated and creamy.

5. Season with salt and pepper to taste. Sprinkle with parsley before serving.

Leftovers: To heat leftovers, melt a tablespoon of butter in a skillet. Add the leftover pasta and cook on low heat while stirring in a tablespoon or two of cream or milk. Stir gently and cook for a few minutes, or until the pasta is heated through.

Spaghetti with Broccoli and Garlic

30-MINUTE · DAIRY-FREE · ONE POT/PAN · VEGETARIAN

Pasta has always been a favorite in our house, and I make it for dinner often. This spaghetti with broccoli and garlic is a good vegetarian dish. It can also be made into a vegan entrée if you swap the butter for more olive oil and serve it without the Parmesan cheese.

Serves: 6
Prep time: 10 minutes
Cook time: 20 minutes

1 pound uncooked spaghetti

2 bunches broccoli, trimmed and cut into florets

2 tablespoons butter

⅓ cup olive oil

4 garlic cloves, minced

1 teaspoon salt

Red pepper flakes

Optional: grated Parmesan cheese

1. In a large pot of water over medium-high heat, boil the spaghetti for 10 to 12 minutes, until al dente (or according to the package directions). Add the broccoli florets the last 3 minutes of cooking. Drain.

2. Melt the butter in the pot over medium heat and add the olive oil. Stir in the garlic and salt. Cook for 2 to 3 minutes, until fragrant. Add the cooked broccoli and spaghetti to the pot and toss well until combined. Season with red pepper to taste.

3. Serve with Parmesan cheese, if desired.

Ingredient Tip: I use garlic often, so there are always a few bulbs in my pantry. Choose bulbs that are firm and have their paper-like skin intact. Do not purchase if they are bruised or have started to sprout. Garlic does not have to be refrigerated, but it can be stored in its skin in a cool, dry place for up to 4 months. For the best quality, I prefer to use it within a month.

Tortellini Caprese

30-MINUTE · VEGETARIAN

Tortellini has a special place in my heart because my grandmother made them from scratch for every holiday. I don't have time to make homemade ones, but I always keep several bags in the freezer. They never let me down when I need a quick and easy dinner.

Serves: 4
Prep time: 5 minutes
Cook time: 25 minutes

1 (1-pound) package frozen cheese tortellini

2 tablespoons olive oil

1 tablespoon crushed garlic

2 cups chopped tomatoes

¾ cup white wine

3 tablespoons chopped fresh basil

8 ounces mozzarella cheese, cut into bite-size pieces

Salt

Red pepper flakes

1. In a large pot of water over high heat, boil the tortellini for 6 minutes, until tender (or according to the package directions). Drain and keep warm in a covered bowl.

2. In a large frying pan, heat the olive oil on medium-high heat. Add the garlic and the tomatoes. Sauté for 5 minutes or until the tomatoes start to soften and the juices start to run. Add the wine and reduce the heat to medium. Cook for 10 minutes or until the liquid starts to evaporate.

3. Mix in the cooked tortellini. Add the chopped basil. Stir gently and cook on low for a few minutes, until the tortellini is well coated with the sauce. Mix in the mozzarella cheese.

4. Season with salt and red pepper to taste before serving.

Easy Variation: Use a 14-ounce can of diced tomatoes instead of the fresh tomatoes. These are convenient to keep in your pantry and will save you a few minutes of prep time.

Caprese Pasta Salad

30-MINUTE · ONE POT/PAN · VEGETARIAN

New Jersey, my home state, has the best tomatoes in the world. Of course, this is only my opinion. But it is a fact that I make this pasta salad once a week during the summer to use up all the delicious tomatoes I grow in my garden. You can make the salad ahead of time and refrigerate it. If the pasta gets too dry, you can always mix in a little extra dressing just before you serve.

Serves: 6
Prep time: 5 minutes
Cook time: 20 minutes

---

1 (12-ounce) box uncooked pasta (rotini, penne, or any medium-size shape)

1 pint cherry tomatoes, halved

8 ounces fresh mozzarella cheese balls, halved

½ cup Simple Italian Vinaigrette (page 166), plus more if needed

Salt

Black pepper

3 tablespoons chopped fresh basil

1. In a large pot of salted water (add 1 teaspoon) over high heat, boil the pasta for 10 to 12 minutes, until al dente (or according to package directions, depending on the shape of pasta). Rinse with cool water in a colander.

2. Place the pasta in a large bowl and stir in the tomatoes, cheese, and Italian vinaigrette. Season with salt and pepper to taste. Sprinkle in the basil right before serving.

Technique Tutorial: To chop basil, first pull the leaves off the stems. Then stack the basil leaves on top of one another and roll them together like a cigar. Thinly slice the rolled basil leaves to form ribbon-like strands. The basil is now ready to use in your salad.

Penne and Chicken à la Vodka

Why go to an Italian restaurant when you can have this chicken and pasta dish on your table in 30 minutes? I always keep homemade marinara sauce in the freezer because my family loves Italian food. This dish is on our menu several times a month.

Serves: 6
Prep time: 5 minutes
Cook time: 25 minutes

1 pound uncooked penne

2 tablespoons olive oil

1 pound chicken tenderloins, cut into bite-size pieces

Salt

Black pepper

½ cup vodka

3 cups Basic Marinara Sauce (page 173)

¾ cup heavy cream

Optional: grated Parmesan cheese, chopped fresh parsley or basil for garnish

1. In a large pot of water over high heat, boil the penne for about 8 minutes, until al dente (or according to the package directions). Drain the pasta and keep warm in a large covered bowl.

2. While the pasta is cooking, heat the olive oil in a large skillet over medium-high heat. Season the chicken with salt and pepper and add it to the pan. Cook for about 3 minutes on each side. The chicken should no longer be pink inside. Add the vodka to the pan and cook for a few minutes, until the liquid is reduced by half. Add the marinara sauce and cook for another 5 minutes, until bubbly.

3. Reduce the heat to low and add the cream. Mix well and cook for 5 more minutes, or until the sauce is fairly thick.

4. Pour the chicken and sauce over the pasta and stir to combine. Season with salt and pepper to taste. Serve with grated Parmesan cheese and garnish with fresh herbs, if desired.

Easy Variation: If you do not have homemade Basic Marinara Sauce in your freezer, your favorite jarred sauce will do.

Sausage and Broccoli Penne Skillet

DAIRY-FREE

This hearty skillet is the perfect weeknight dinner. It includes pasta, vegetables, and meat for a complete meal. Every time you make this recipe, the compliments will be flying.

Serves: 6
Prep time: 10 minutes
Cook time: 30 minutes

12 ounces uncooked penne

1 head broccoli, stalks trimmed and florets cut into bite-size pieces

2 tablespoons olive oil

8 ounces Italian sausage (3 or 4 links), cut into 2-inch pieces

1 tablespoon minced garlic

1 (14-ounce) can diced tomatoes

1 tablespoon dried Italian seasoning

Salt

Black pepper

Optional: grated Parmesan cheese

1. In a large pot of salted water (add 1 teaspoon) over high heat, boil the penne for about 10 minutes, until al dente (or according to the package directions). During the last 2 minutes of cooking, add the broccoli.

2. Drain, reserving ½ cup of the pasta water. Keep the penne warm in a covered bowl.

3. While the pasta is cooking, heat the olive oil over medium heat in a large skillet or frying pan. Add the sausage and cook until brown, 8 to 10 minutes.

4. Add the garlic, tomatoes, and Italian seasoning. Cook for a few minutes, until the sauce is bubbling. Turn the heat to low, cover, and cook an additional 10 minutes.

5. Add the cooked pasta, broccoli, and reserved pasta water. Stir well and cook for about 3 minutes, or until the water evaporates and the sauce thickens. Season with salt and pepper to taste.

6. Sprinkle with Parmesan cheese before serving, if desired.

Technique Tutorial: *Al dente* means "firm to the bite," or pasta that is not overcooked. To cook pasta al dente, taste the pasta when it gets close to the estimated cooking time. It should have the texture of a firm stick of gum.

Southwest Mac and Beef Skillet

30-MINUTE · DAIRY-FREE

I didn't grow up on Hamburger Helper, but lots of my friends did. This is the homemade version, with no powdered cheese. Everyone could use a comforting bowl of macaroni and beef, and it's so much better when you make it yourself with real ingredients.

Serves: 6
Prep time: 5 minutes
Cook time: 25 minutes

---

12 ounces uncooked elbow macaroni

1 tablespoon olive oil

1 pound lean ground beef

1 small onion, peeled and diced

2 tablespoons chili powder

1 (14-ounce) can fire-roasted diced tomatoes with green chilies

1 (15-ounce) can red kidney beans, rinsed and drained

Salt

Optional: shredded Cheddar cheese

1. In a large pot of water over high heat, boil the macaroni for 8 to 10 minutes, until tender (or according to the package directions). Drain, reserving ½ cup of the pasta water.

2. While the pasta is cooking, heat the olive oil on medium-high heat in a large skillet. Add the ground beef and cook for 5 minutes or until the beef starts to brown. Stir with a wooden spoon while it's cooking to break up the chunks. Sprinkle the beef with the chili powder and add the tomatoes. Bring to a simmer, reduce the heat to medium, cover, and cook for 10 minutes.

3. Add the beans, mix well, and cook for another few minutes, or until the sauce is thickened. Stir in the cooked macaroni and combine well.

4. Remove the pan from the heat and season with salt to taste. Garnish with lots of Cheddar cheese, if desired, before serving.

Simple Swap: You can swap any other canned beans for the red beans, depending on your preference. I like to make this recipe with white beans or black beans.

Spicy Sesame Noodles

There is no need to order Chinese takeout when you can make sesame noodles at home. These versatile noodles can be served warm or cold. Sesame seeds are optional, but I love to sprinkle a few tablespoons on the noodles when I serve them.

Serves: 6
Prep time: 5 minutes
Cook time: 20 minutes

---

1 pound uncooked spaghetti or fettuccine

¼ cup sweet Asian chili sauce

6 tablespoons soy sauce

2 tablespoons sesame oil

½ teaspoon garlic powder

2 scallions, finely chopped

Red pepper flakes

Optional: 3 tablespoons sesame seeds

1. In a large pot of water over medium-high heat, boil the spaghetti for about 10 minutes, until al dente (or according to the package directions). Drain and transfer to a big serving bowl.

2. In a small bowl, whisk together the chili sauce, soy sauce, sesame oil, and garlic powder. Mix the warm spaghetti with the sauce until it is well coated.

3. Toss the noodles with the scallions and season with red pepper to taste. Sprinkle with sesame seeds, if desired. Serve warm or cold.

Leftovers: These noodles are great the next day because the flavors blend together well. Just store leftovers in the refrigerator in an airtight container. Take them out of the fridge 30 minutes before serving.

Cranberry and Feta Quinoa

30-MINUTE · GLUTEN-FREE · ONE POT/PAN · VEGETARIAN

Quinoa is a healthy grain-like food that contains more protein than pasta or rice. My daughter is a vegetarian, so for her this makes a great meatless dish. I also serve this as a side to poultry or fish but find myself eating the leftovers for lunch the next day.

Serves: 4
Prep time: 5 minutes
Cook time: 25 minutes

1 cup uncooked quinoa

2 cups water

½ cup sweetened dried cranberries

⅓ cup chopped toasted walnuts

½ cup crumbled feta cheese

⅓ cup Simple Italian Vinaigrette (page 166), or bottled dressing

Salt

Black pepper

Optional: 2 tablespoons chopped fresh parsley

1. In a medium saucepan, add the quinoa and water. Cook on medium heat and bring to a boil. Turn the heat down to low and simmer for 10 to 15 minutes, or until the water is almost all evaporated. Remove from the heat and cover. Let it rest for about 5 minutes, or until the quinoa is tender. Fluff and separate the grains with a fork.

2. Transfer the quinoa to a bowl and let cool for 10 minutes. Mix in the cranberries, walnuts, and feta cheese. Toss with the dressing. Season with salt and pepper to taste.

3. Garnish with parsley, if desired. This will give it more color and flavor but is not necessary.

Prep Tip: Quinoa can be rinsed in a colander before cooking to remove its natural coating and give it a less earthy flavor. I prefer the strong, nutty flavor and it's less work for me, so I do not rinse it. It's a personal preference that's up to your taste. You can also look for prerinsed quinoa, which is sold in many grocery stores. Just look on the label.

Cheesy Quinoa-Stuffed Peppers

GLUTEN-FREE · VEGETARIAN

If you want vegetarian comfort food with a Southwestern flair, this recipe is for you! While these peppers take close to an hour to cook, the oven does most of the work, not you. So relax with a glass of wine while you are waiting for dinner to be done.

Serves: 6
Prep time: 10 minutes
Cook time: 60 minutes

Nonstick cooking spray

1 tablespoon olive oil

1 medium onion, peeled and chopped

2 cups Three-Minute Blender Salsa (page 168), or your favorite salsa, divided

2 cups cooked quinoa

2½ cups shredded Cheddar cheese, divided

3 medium red bell peppers, seeded and halved lengthwise with the inside ribs removed

1. Preheat the oven to 375°F. Spray a rimmed baking sheet with nonstick cooking spray

2. In a large frying pan, heat the oil over medium heat and sauté the onion for 5 minutes or until it starts to soften. Add 1½ cups of salsa and simmer on low for 10 minutes.

3. Add the cooked quinoa to the pan, stir well, and cook until bubbly.

4. Add 2 cups of cheese to the pan and mix well. Remove from the heat.

5. Lay the peppers cut-side up on the baking sheet. Spoon the filling into the pepper halves. Cover the peppers loosely with a sheet of foil.

6. Bake for about 45 minutes, or until the peppers are tender. Sprinkle the remaining ½ cup of cheese over the filling of the peppers and bake for 5 more minutes, or until the cheese melts. Serve the peppers with the remaining ½ cup of salsa on the side.

Technique Tutorial: To cook quinoa, bring 2 cups of water to a boil. Stir in 1 cup of uncooked quinoa (that has been rinsed in a colander, if desired), and turn the heat down to low. Cover and simmer for about 15 minutes, or until the water is absorbed. Fluff and separate the grains with a fork. This will make 3 cups cooked. It's perfect to make in advance and keep in the fridge for when you need it in a recipe.

Salsa Verde Rice and Beans

30-MINUTE · DAIRY-FREE · GLUTEN-FREE · ONE POT/PAN · VEGETARIAN

Rice and beans are inexpensive to make, and the salsa verde provides lots of flavor. This works as a side dish or a good vegan or vegetarian entrée. I always keep all the ingredients in my pantry so I can make this as a last-minute dinner any time.

Serves: 4
Prep time: 5 minutes
Cook time: 25 minutes

---

1 tablespoon olive oil

¼ cup finely chopped onion

1 cup uncooked long-grain white rice

2 cups vegetable broth

1 teaspoon chili powder

1 cup store-bought salsa verde

1 (15-ounce) can red beans, rinsed and drained

Salt

Black pepper

1. Heat the olive oil over medium-high heat in a medium saucepan. Sauté the onion for 4 to 5 minutes, until it softens and begins to brown.

2. Add the uncooked rice and sauté for 2 minutes, stirring constantly. Pour the broth into the pot. Mix in the chili powder and salsa verde. Bring the mixture to a boil, then cover.

3. Reduce the heat to low and simmer for 20 minutes, or until the rice is tender.

4. Mix in the beans and cover again. Remove the pot from the heat and let the rice and beans stand for a few minutes with the lid on. Fluff the rice and beans with a fork and add salt and pepper to taste before serving.

Technique Tutorial: To fluff the rice, use a fork to mix it up a bit, separate the grains, and remove any lumps to give it a nice light texture. Do not use a spoon, as it could mash or bruise the rice.

Oven-Baked Mushroom Risotto

GLUTEN-FREE

Don't be intimidated to cook risotto! The oven does all the work in this easier version. I love the taste that chicken broth gives this dish, but you can make it vegetarian by substituting vegetable broth instead.

Serves: 6
Prep time: 5 minutes
Cook time: 1 hour

2 tablespoons salted butter

8 ounces sliced mushrooms

1½ cups arborio rice

4 cups chicken broth

¾ cup grated Parmesan cheese

3 tablespoons chopped fresh parsley

Salt

Black pepper

1. Preheat the oven to 350°F.

2. In a large skillet, heat the butter over medium heat. Add the mushrooms and sauté for 4 to 5 minutes, or until they are soft.

3. Spoon the mushrooms and any liquid into a medium casserole dish. Mix in the rice and chicken broth. Stir well.

4. Cover and place the dish in the center of the oven. Bake for about 50 minutes, or until the rice is tender and most of the liquid is absorbed. It should be creamy, not dry. If it is too dry, add a little extra heated broth. Start by adding ½ cup and adjust if necessary.

5. Remove the risotto from the oven. Stir in the Parmesan cheese and chopped parsley.

6. Season with salt and pepper to taste.

Ingredient Tip: Arborio rice is a short-grain, plump, high-starch rice that becomes creamy when cooked. It can be found in the rice and pasta section in your grocery store. Never rinse this type of rice before cooking because the starch content would be compromised and you would not get a creamy texture.

Chapter 9

Seafood and Fish

Lemon and White Wine Shrimp Cocktail

30-MINUTE · DAIRY-FREE · GLUTEN-FREE · ONE POT/PAN

This elegant appetizer is ready in 15 minutes, so there is no need to wait for a fancy party to make it. Shrimp is often on sale at the grocery store, and I make sure to always take advantage of that. We enjoy this recipe as a simple appetizer at home on a weeknight or the weekend. These shrimp can be made one day ahead of time and chilled in an airtight container in the refrigerator. Do not store leftover shrimp for more than two days.

Serves: 4 to 6
Prep time: 5 minutes
Cook time: 10 minutes

---

1 tablespoon olive oil

2 garlic cloves, crushed

1 pound large shrimp, peeled, deveined, tail left on

½ large lemon, sliced, with extra wedges for serving

½ cup white wine

1 tablespoon Cajun seasoning

1 tablespoon dried Italian seasoning

Optional: shrimp cocktail sauce

1. Heat the olive oil over medium heat in a large frying pan. Add the garlic and shrimp. Cook for about 2 minutes, or until the garlic starts to be fragrant.

2. Add the lemon slices and wine, and sprinkle the Cajun and Italian seasonings on top. Stir the shrimp well.

3. Cook for about 3 to 4 minutes, or until the shrimp turn pink. Drain and transfer to a bowl. Serve warm or cold, with extra lemon wedges and cocktail sauce, if desired.

Technique Tutorial: The easiest way to work with shrimp is to buy it already peeled and deveined. If you decide to buy uncleaned shrimp, first go underneath to where the legs are attached and dig your thumb inside to release the shell. Peel the whole shell off, then run the tip of a paring knife down the middle of the back of the shrimp. Pull out the gray vein and your shrimp are ready to use. You can leave the tail on or cut it off.

Sheet Pan Fajita Shrimp

30-MINUTE · GLUTEN-FREE · ONE POT/PAN

These savory shrimp with peppers and onions are very much like the shrimp fajitas you can order in Mexican restaurants. They are great served with corn or flour tortillas and condiments such as salsa, shredded cheese, and sour cream. Making these fajitas at home can save you money.

Serves: 6
Prep time: 5 minutes
Cook time: 20 minutes

2 tablespoons chili powder

1 tablespoon sea salt

2 medium red bell peppers, seeded and cut into 2-inch strips

1 medium yellow or green bell pepper, seeded and cut into 2-inch strips

1 large onion, peeled, halved, and thinly sliced

3 tablespoons olive oil, divided

1½ pounds shrimp, peeled and deveined

1. Preheat the oven to 400°F. Line a baking sheet with parchment paper.

2. In a small bowl, mix together the chili powder and salt. Set aside.

3. In a large bowl, toss together the bell peppers and onions. Drizzle with 1½ teaspoons of olive oil and half the chili powder mixture. Toss to coat evenly.

4. Spread the seasoned peppers and onions on the baking sheet and bake for 15 minutes.

5. While the vegetables are baking, place the shrimp in the same large bowl you tossed the peppers and onions in. Drizzle the remaining 1½ teaspoons of olive oil over the shrimp and sprinkle with the remaining chili powder mixture. Mix well.

6. After the peppers and onions have been in the oven for 15 minutes, remove the baking sheet and add the shrimp in an even layer. Return to the oven and bake for an additional 6 to 8 minutes, or until the shrimp are pink and tender.

Ingredient Tip: Keep a bag of peeled, deveined shrimp in your freezer for convenience. They must be defrosted before you can cook them. Place the frozen shrimp in a colander under cold running water for 10 minutes and they will be ready to use.

Lemon Butter and Chive Pan-Seared Scallops

Scallops are one of my favorite special occasion dinners. The best part about them is that they take under 15 minutes to cook. You will spend more time eating and relaxing at dinner than you will spend cooking. Chives are great with the scallops, but other fresh herbs, like basil or parsley, are nice variations.

Serves: 4
Prep time: 5 minutes
Cook time: 10 minutes

---

1 pound large dry or diver scallops

Salt

Black pepper

3 tablespoons salted butter, divided

2 tablespoons freshly squeezed lemon juice

2 tablespoons chopped fresh chives

Optional: chopped lettuce leaves or other greens

1. Pat the scallops dry with paper towels. Season to taste with salt and pepper.

2. Heat 1 tablespoon of butter in a large skillet over medium-high heat. When the butter starts to foam, add the scallops to the pan and cook for 2 to 3 minutes on each side, or until they are nicely seared and the center of the scallop looks translucent. Remove from the pan and keep warm.

3. Add the remaining 2 tablespoons of butter to the pan and turn the heat to medium. Cook until the butter starts to foam and turns slightly brown. Add the lemon juice and chives. Whisk the mixture and return the scallops to the pan.

4. Spoon the sauce over them and heat for another minute while coating with sauce. Transfer to a plate and garnish with lettuce or greens, if desired.

Ingredient Tip: When you're buying scallops, get the biggest ones you can find and afford. Also look for dry or diver scallops. They are a bit more expensive but contain no preservatives, so very little liquid is released when cooking. This means you'll get a nicely seared crust.

Sweet Chili and Soy Baked Salmon

30-MINUTE · DAIRY-FREE · ONE POT/PAN

Salmon is both healthy and delicious, so it is on my dinner menu often. This Asian-inspired sauce packs in the flavor. Soy sauce typically has gluten, but there are gluten-free brands at your grocery store, if that's an issue. Sweet Asian chili sauce is a sweet but savory, not-too-hot sauce you can find in the Asian foods aisle of many supermarkets. I like to serve this dish with some plain rice and Spicy Cucumber Salad (page 49) to make it a complete dinner.

Serves: 4
Prep time: 5 minutes
Cook time: 20 minutes

---

2 tablespoons soy sauce

2 tablespoons sweet Asian chili sauce

1 tablespoon rice vinegar

4 salmon fillets (about 1 ¼ pounds total), skin on

½ teaspoon salt

¼ teaspoon black pepper

Optional: 2 tablespoons chopped fresh cilantro for garnish

1. Preheat the oven to 375°F. Line a baking sheet with parchment paper.

2. In a small bowl, mix together the soy sauce, chili sauce, and vinegar. Set aside.

3. Season the salmon fillets with salt and pepper. Place on the baking sheet skin-side down. Spoon the sauce over the salmon.

4. Bake for about 15 minutes, or until the fish is tender and cooked through. It should be light pink and flake when touched with a fork. Garnish with chopped cilantro, if desired.

Easy Variation: If you are in a hurry, you can substitute ⅓ cup bottled teriyaki sauce instead of mixing together the soy sauce, chili sauce, and vinegar.

Pan-Roasted Halibut Piccata

This halibut is a great way to get a quick dinner on the table. I serve it with noodles or mashed potatoes on the side. And when dinner is over, there is only one pan to clean.

Serves: 4
Prep time: 5 minutes
Cook time: 20 minutes

2 tablespoons olive oil

½ teaspoon salt

¼ teaspoon black pepper

4 (6-ounce) halibut steaks

1 cup low-sodium chicken broth

Juice of 1 lemon

3 tablespoons brined capers, rinsed

4 tablespoons chopped fresh parsley

2 tablespoons salted butter

1 lemon, thinly sliced

1. Preheat the oven to 350°F.

2. Heat the oil in a large ovenproof pan over medium-high heat. Sprinkle the salt and pepper on the halibut. Sear the fish for about 2 minutes on each side, or until the fish just starts to turn golden. Transfer the fish from the pan to a plate.

3. Add the broth, lemon juice, capers, and parsley to the pan. Cook for a few minutes, until the sauce begins to evaporate a bit and thicken. Add the butter to the pan and stir well.

4. Put the fish back in the pan and spoon some of the sauce on top. Place the pan in the oven and cook for 7 to 8 minutes, or until the fish is cooked through and easily flakes with a fork.

5. Serve the fish with the sauce spooned over it. Serve with the lemon slices.

Ingredient Tip: Capers are pickled flower buds, and can be found in jars in the pickle and olive section or Italian food aisle of your grocery store. If you can't find them, you can substitute 3 tablespoons of chopped green olives instead.

Crispy Panfried Cod

30-MINUTE · DAIRY-FREE · ONE POT/PAN

I come from a Catholic family, and due to religious beliefs, my family never ate meat on Fridays during Lent (the season leading up to Easter). So fish was on the dinner table almost every Friday night. While I don't really continue the tradition, I do love to make this fish for dinner. It's very kid-friendly, and my family has always loved it.

Serves: 6
Prep time: 15 minutes
Cook time: 10 minutes

6 cod fillets (about 1½ to 2 pounds total)

½ cup all-purpose flour

1 tablespoon Cajun or Old Bay seasoning

2 eggs, beaten

1 to 2 cups seasoned panko breadcrumbs

¼ to ½ cup olive oil

Salt

Black pepper

1. Pat the cod fillets dry with paper towels. Set aside.

2. Line up 3 shallow bowls or plates right next to one another. Fill the first one with the flour mixed with the Cajun seasoning. Fill the second one with the eggs, and the third one with the breadcrumbs.

3. Dip each fish fillet in the seasoned flour, making sure both sides are coated. Then dip it in the egg, and finally, press the fish into the panko breadcrumbs, making sure the fillet gets a nice, even coating.

4. In a large skillet over medium heat, heat enough olive oil to cover the bottom of pan. Carefully add the fish fillets to the pan and cook for about 3 minutes, or until the cod is golden brown. Flip gently with a spatula and cook for another 2 to 3 minutes, or until the fish flakes with a fork. Remove the fish from the pan and season with salt and pepper to taste.

5. If all the fish fillets do not fit in your pan, they can be cooked in two batches. Just add a little more oil to the pan, if needed.

Simple Swap: You can substitute another white fish, such as tilapia or haddock, for cod.

Spinach Baked Tilapia

30-MINUTE · ONE POT/PAN

If you're not sure you like to eat fish, tilapia is a good one to try. It is a mild-tasting, white, flaky fish. Since it's very mild, this was always my go-to fish dinner that I served when my kids were younger.

Serves: 4
Prep time: 5 minutes
Cook time: 25 minutes

Nonstick cooking spray

10 ounces fresh
baby spinach

1 tablespoon olive oil

¼ teaspoon sea salt, plus
more to taste

4 large tilapia fillets (about
1¼ pounds total)

Juice of ½ lemon

1 tablespoon salted
butter, melted

½ cup seasoned
breadcrumbs

1 tablespoon dried parsley

Salt

Black pepper

Optional: lemon wedges
for serving

1. Preheat the oven to 350°F. Spray a large baking dish with nonstick cooking spray.

2. Spread the spinach out in the baking dish and toss with the oil and salt. Lay the fish fillets on top. Drizzle the lemon juice and butter on top of the fish. Sprinkle with the breadcrumbs.

3. Bake for 15 to 20 minutes, or until the fish flakes with a fork. Turn the oven to broil for 1 or 2 minutes so the breadcrumbs on top turn golden.

4. Before serving, sprinkle with the parsley and season with salt and pepper to taste. Serve with extra lemon wedges, if desired.

Ingredient tip: You can buy frozen bags of tilapia to keep in your freezer. To safely defrost them, place the fillets in a shallow bowl, cover, and leave in the refrigerator overnight. If you are in a rush, the fillets can be placed in a resealable plastic bag and submerged in a bowl of cold water. Replace the water after 15 minutes. The fish should defrost in under 30 minutes.

Southwest Tilapia Tacos

GLUTEN-FREE

I could eat fish tacos three times a week and never get tired of them. These tacos are made healthier than typical fried ones as the tilapia fillets are panfried in just a little bit of olive oil. Feel free to substitute another type of fish, such as flounder or cod.

Serves: 4
Prep time: 20 minutes
Cook time: 15 minutes

4 tilapia fillets
(1 pound total)

1 tablespoon Southwest
or taco seasoning, or
chili powder

2 tablespoons olive
oil, divided

2 cups coleslaw mix

2 tablespoons chopped
fresh cilantro, plus more
for garnish

Juice of 1 large lime

Salt

Pepper

8 corn tortillas, warmed

¾ cup Spicy Avocado
Cream (page 170) or
store-bought guacamole

1. Rinse the fish fillets and pat dry with paper towels. Sprinkle the seasoning on both sides of the fish.

2. Heat a large skillet over medium-high heat. Add 1½ tablespoons of olive oil to coat the pan, then add the fish fillets. Cook for 2 minutes on each side, or until the outside is golden and the fish is cooked through. Transfer the fish to a plate and break it up into 8 pieces.

3. In a medium bowl, mix together the slaw mix, cilantro, remaining ½ tablespoon of olive oil, and the lime juice. Season with salt and pepper to taste.

4. Assemble the tacos by placing some slaw mix on each tortilla, then a piece of fish. Top with a spoonful or two of Spicy Avocado Cream, and garnish with extra cilantro, if desired.

Technique Tutorial: To warm the tortillas, place them in two stacks of four and wrap them in aluminum foil. Put them in a preheated 350°F oven for 10 to 15 minutes or until heated through.

Chapter 10

Chicken and Turkey

Harvest Chicken Salad

30-MINUTE · DAIRY-FREE · GLUTEN-FREE · NO-COOK

I distinctly remember the first time I had chicken salad with grapes in it because it was so good. Now I never make chicken salad any other way. This recipe is equally good whether you use chopped turkey or chopped chicken.

Serves: 6
Prep time: 15 minutes

3 cups shredded or chopped cooked chicken

3 celery stalks, finely diced

½ cup mayonnaise

1 cup grapes, halved or sliced

1 tablespoon seasoned rice vinegar

Salt

Black pepper

1. Put the chicken, celery, mayonnaise, grapes, and rice vinegar in a medium bowl.

2. Mix well and season with salt and pepper to taste.

Ingredient Tip: Use a store-bought rotisserie chicken or precooked chicken sold in packages in the grocery store. You could also make Simple Roasted Chicken (page 117) and just use your hands to pull the leftover meat off the bones for this recipe.

Simple Roasted Chicken

DAIRY FREE · GLUTEN FREE · ONE POT/PAN

Roasting chicken does not get any easier than this. This recipe can serve as your main course for dinner, or you can make it any time you need precooked chicken. Just cool the chicken and use your hands to pull it off the bone, then chop or shred it. It's now ready to use in soups, sandwiches, and salads.

Serves: 6
Prep time: 10 minutes
Cook time: 50 minutes

1 (3- to 4-pound) chicken, cut into 8 pieces (2 drumsticks, 2 thighs, 2 wings, 2 breasts)

2 tablespoons olive oil

1 to 2 tablespoons seasoned salt

1 tablespoon dried Italian seasoning

Optional: Basic BBQ Sauce (page 171)

1. Preheat the oven to 400°F.

2. Pat the chicken parts dry with paper towels, then brush the skin of the chicken with the olive oil. Sprinkle with the seasoned salt and Italian seasoning. Place the pieces in a shallow baking pan, with the biggest pieces in the middle.

3. Roast the chicken for 30 minutes, then reduce the heat to 350°F. Roast for about 15 minutes more, or until an instant-read thermometer placed in the thickest part of a chicken piece reads 165°F. (It's best to test more than one piece.) If you do not have an instant-read thermometer, the chicken should be done when the juices run clear and the chicken is no longer pink inside. Use a paring knife to cut a small slit in the chicken to get an idea of what the meat inside looks like.

4. Serve with barbecue sauce, if desired.

Prep Tip: In the meat department of your grocery store, you can buy a whole chicken that has been cut up and packaged. Or, if you prefer, you can buy a whole chicken and ask the butcher to cut it into 8 pieces.

Sweet and Spicy Baked Chicken Wings

GLUTEN-FREE · ONE POT/PAN

My family loves ordering wings when we go out, but I also like making them. Restaurant wings are typically deep-fried; baking chicken wings seals in the flavor and cuts down the fat and calories. I promise, these are still extra delicious. You can use this recipe to make different-flavor wings, too. Instead of the pepper sauce, honey, and butter, toss the wings with ½ cup of your favorite barbecue or teriyaki sauce.

Serves: 4
Prep time: 10 minutes
Cook time: 45 minutes

Nonstick cooking spray

3 pounds chicken wings, tips removed, flats and drumettes separated

1 tablespoon olive oil

1 tablespoon seasoned salt

3 tablespoons cayenne pepper sauce

3 tablespoons honey

2 tablespoons butter, melted

Optional: ranch or blue cheese dressing, chopped fresh herbs

1. Preheat the oven to 425°F. Spray a large rimmed baking sheet with nonstick cooking spray.

2. In a large bowl, toss the wing pieces with the olive oil and seasoned salt. Spread the chicken out on the baking sheet.

3. Roast for 20 minutes, then turn the wings. Roast 20 to 25 minutes more, or until the wings are crispy.

4. In a large bowl, whisk together the pepper sauce, honey, and butter. Toss the baked wings in the sauce until well coated. Serve with dressing on the side, if desired. These wings can also be garnished with chopped fresh herbs if desired.

Ingredient Tip: There are three parts to a chicken wing. The tips are the small, skinny end and are usually discarded. The drumettes look like small chicken legs, and the flats are the parts in between that contain several bones. You can buy frozen chicken wings in big bags with the tips already trimmed off and the flats and drumettes separated. Defrost overnight in the refrigerator before cooking. To separate whole fresh wings, cut the wings between the joints separating the tips, flats, and drumettes.

Pan-Roasted Lemon and Thyme Chicken Thighs

DAIRY-FREE · GLUTEN-FREE · ONE POT/PAN

When I make whole roasted chicken, everyone wants the drumsticks or thighs. My family prefers dark meat, so this dish makes everyone happy. The fresh lemon really brings the flavor of this dish to another level.

Serves: 6
Prep time: 5 minutes
Cook time: 40 minutes

---

1 tablespoon olive oil

6 bone-in chicken thighs

Salt

Black pepper

1 cup low-sodium chicken broth

1 tablespoon dried thyme

Juice of 1 lemon

1 medium lemon, sliced

1. Preheat the oven to 350°F.

2. Heat the olive oil in a large ovenproof frying pan over medium-high heat. Sprinkle the chicken with salt and pepper to taste. Add the chicken to the pan, skin-side down, and cook for about 4 minutes, or until the skin is crispy and golden brown.

3. Turn the chicken pieces over and cook for another 4 minutes, then transfer them to a plate.

4. Add the chicken broth, thyme, and lemon juice to the pan. Bring the mixture to a boil and add the chicken back to the pan, skin-side up. Scatter the lemon slices around the chicken in the pan.

5. Place the pan in the oven and roast for about 30 minutes, or until the chicken is cooked through and the juices run clear when you prick a piece with a fork. The chicken should no longer be pink inside. If you have an instant-read thermometer, it should read 165°F or above.

Technique Tutorial: An easy way to juice a lemon is to put it in the microwave for 20 to 30 seconds. Roll it back and forth a little along your kitchen counter, then cut it in half, poke out the seeds with the tip of a paring knife, and squeeze the juice out into a small bowl. Microwaving and rolling will soften the lemon and get the juices flowing, to produce the most juice.

One-Pan Chicken Cordon Bleu

30-MINUTE · GLUTEN-FREE · ONE POT/PAN

Despite its French name, Chicken Cordon Bleu originated in the United States in the 1960s. It was a trendy adaptation of an older French dish that used veal. It is still quite popular, so I decided to create the easiest version ever. You'll want to put this one-pan dish on your dinner table often.

Serves: 6
Prep time: 10 minutes
Cook time: 15 minutes

4 thin chicken cutlets (about 1 pound total)

1 teaspoon seasoned salt

1 to 2 tablespoons olive oil

½ cup low-sodium chicken broth

2 tablespoons half-and-half

1 teaspoon dried parsley

4 thin slices deli ham

4 slices Swiss cheese

1. Sprinkle both sides of the chicken with the seasoned salt.

2. Heat enough olive oil to coat the bottom of a large skillet over medium heat. Add the chicken and cook for 2 to 3 minutes on each side, or until the chicken is golden.

3. Remove the chicken from the pan, reduce the heat to medium, and add the chicken broth, half-and-half, and dried parsley to the pan. Scrape the pan with a spatula and stir well to deglaze. Cook for a few minutes, until the sauce starts to simmer.

4. Return the chicken to the skillet and spoon some sauce on top of each piece. Top each with a slice of ham and a slice of cheese. Cover the skillet with a lid and cook on low for 3 to 4 minutes, or until the cheese melts.

5. Serve the sauce with the chicken.

Simple Swap: Substitute your favorite type of cheese for the Swiss cheese. This dish is good with mozzarella, provolone, or white Cheddar cheese.

Bruschetta Chicken Cutlets

Breaded chicken cutlets have always been a staple in my house. (Make sure the breadcrumbs don't contain cheese if you want this recipe to be dairy-free.) These are topped with a bruschetta mixture, a juicy tomato salad that my husband loves. Feel free to change the toppings—my family loves roasted peppers, sautéed spinach, or just melted cheese on top.

Serves: 6
Prep time: 10 minutes
Cook time: 15 minutes

2 large plum
tomatoes, chopped

2 teaspoons
balsamic vinegar

4 tablespoons olive
oil, divided

2 teaspoons dried basil

Salt

Black pepper

1 egg

3 tablespoons water

2/3 cup Italian-style panko
breadcrumbs

6 thin chicken cutlets (about
1¼ pounds total)

1. In a medium bowl, mix together the tomatoes, vinegar, 1 tablespoon of olive oil, and basil. Season with salt and pepper to taste. Set aside.

2. In a shallow bowl, beat together the egg and water. Put the breadcrumbs in another shallow bowl.

3. Dip each chicken cutlet into the egg mixture, then the breadcrumbs, until all are coated.

4. Heat the remaining 3 tablespoons of olive oil in a large skillet over medium heat. Add the coated chicken to the pan and cook for 4 to 6 minutes on each side, or until the chicken is golden brown and no longer pink inside. Remove the chicken from the pan.

5. Top each cutlet with an equal amount of the tomato mixture.

Leftovers: I like to make an extra batch of these chicken cutlets to serve for lunch the next day. Cook the cutlets and refrigerate them in an airtight container. Reheat them on a baking sheet in a preheated 350°F oven for about 10 minutes. While they're heating, make the tomato bruschetta topping (which is best eaten fresh). This chicken is also great on a nice crusty Italian roll. My husband even likes to eat the leftovers cold.

Curry-Spiced Chicken Kabobs

GLUTEN-FREE · ONE POT/PAN

I never tried Indian food until I moved to a place right down the street from a great little Indian restaurant. The chef made delicious tandoori chicken that I would eat with wonderful, fluffy Indian bread. This recipe is inspired by that restaurant, and I love to eat this chicken with fresh pita bread.

Serves: 4 to 6
Prep time: 15 minutes, plus 1 hour to marinate
Cook time: 25 minutes

¼ cup plain Greek yogurt

2 teaspoons curry powder

Juice of 1 lemon

1 teaspoon garlic powder

1 teaspoon salt

¼ teaspoon cayenne pepper, or more, depending on how spicy you like the chicken

2 tablespoons chopped fresh cilantro, plus more for garnish

1¼ pounds boneless, skinless chicken breast, cut into 1- to 2-inch cubes

1. Mix together the yogurt, curry powder, lemon juice, garlic powder, salt, cayenne pepper, and cilantro in a large bowl. Add the chicken and coat well. Put the chicken in a large zipper-top bag and let it marinate in the fridge for at least 1 hour or up to overnight.

2. Preheat the oven to 400°F. Line a rimmed baking sheet with parchment paper or spray it with nonstick cooking spray.

3. Prepare the kabobs by threading the chicken onto 6 wooden or metal skewers. Discard any marinade in the bag.

4. Place the kabobs on the baking sheet and bake for 10 minutes. Turn the kabobs over and bake for another 10 to 15 minutes, or until the chicken is no longer pink inside. Garnish with more chopped cilantro before serving.

Prep Tip: If you are using wooden skewers, soak them in water first so that they don't burn when the food is cooking. I like using a tall glass to soak them in. Make sure to flip them so that both ends of the skewers get soaked in the water. You can also soak them in a long, deep pan, like a loaf pan, if you have one.

Slow Cooker Lemon Roast Chicken

DAIRY-FREE · GLUTEN-FREE · ONE POT/PAN · SLOW COOKER

Whole roasted chicken has a special place in my heart, as it always reminds me of a family dinner. This chicken is cooked in the slow cooker while you are going about your day. Trust me when I say your house will smell delicious! You can also make this chicken in the oven if you do not have a slow cooker. Season the chicken according to the instructions, then rub it with 2 tablespoons of olive oil. Place the chicken in a roasting pan and roast in a preheated 425°F oven for 75 to 90 minutes, or until the chicken is fully cooked.

Serves: 6
Prep time: 10 minutes
Cook time: 6 to 8 hours

1 tablespoon seasoned salt

1 teaspoon black pepper

1 teaspoon garlic powder

1 tablespoon dried Italian seasoning

1 whole roasting or frying chicken (4 to 5 pounds)

3 large carrots, peeled and cut into 1-inch pieces

2 medium onions, peeled and cut into quarters

2 lemons, cut into quarters

1. In a small bowl, mix together the seasoned salt, pepper, garlic powder, and Italian seasoning.

2. Remove the giblets and anything else inside the chicken. Rinse and dry with paper towels. Rub the seasoning mixture all over the chicken, pushing some under the skin.

3. Put the carrots and onions on the bottom of the slow cooker. Place the chicken (breast-side up) on top of the vegetables and tuck in the wings and legs. Squeeze the juice from 4 of the lemon quarters all over the outside of the chicken. Put the remaining 4 lemon quarters inside the cavity of the chicken.

4. Cook the chicken for at least 6 hours on high, after which you can start periodically checking for doneness. The chicken is done when an instant-read thermometer stuck in the thickest part of the chicken reads 165°F. If you do not have one, the chicken is fully cooked when you slice the skin between the leg and the breast and the juices run clear. The juices should not be pink.

5. You can transfer the chicken to a rimmed baking sheet and put it under the broiler for a few minutes, if you would like the skin to be crispy.

Leftovers: Chicken stock can be made from the leftover carcass. Just put it in a large pot filled with water. Add some vegetables, salt, and pepper. Bring the pot to a boil, then let it simmer, covered, on low heat for 2 hours; then strain it through a colander. Store the broth in airtight containers in your fridge or freezer.

Slow Cooker BBQ Pulled Chicken

DAIRY-FREE · FREEZER-FRIENDLY · GLUTEN-FREE · ONE POT/PAN · SLOW COOKER

My family loves this no-fail recipe. I serve this chicken with flour tortillas or potato rolls and coleslaw on the side. This chicken is excellent to add to quesadillas, too. I love my homemade Basic BBQ Sauce, but feel free to use your favorite store-bought sauce to make things even easier.

Serves: 6
Prep time: 5 minutes
Cook time: 4 to 6 hours

2 pounds (3 or 4) boneless, skinless chicken breasts

Salt

Black pepper

1 cup Basic BBQ Sauce (page 171), plus more for serving

½ cup apple juice

1. Season the chicken with salt and pepper. Place the chicken breasts on the bottom of a slow cooker set to high heat.

2. In a small bowl, mix together the barbecue sauce and the apple juice. Pour it over the chicken.

3. Cook on high for about 4 hours, or 6 hours on low, until the chicken is very tender.

4. Transfer the chicken to a cutting board and pull it apart using two forks while it is still warm. Place the chicken back in the slow cooker and mix with the sauce.

5. Serve with extra barbecue sauce, if desired.

Easy Variation: To cook this on the stove rather than in a slow cooker, put the seasoned chicken in a medium saucepan with the barbecue sauce and apple juice. Cover and cook on medium heat for 20 to 30 minutes, or until the chicken is tender when you stick a fork in it. Use two forks to pull the chicken apart, or chop it up, then put it back in the pan and simmer on low, uncovered, for about 5 minutes, until the sauce is the consistency you want it to be. You can add a little water for thinner sauce.

Fajita Chicken Tacos

ONE POT/PAN

Half my family prefers tacos while the other half prefers fajitas. This recipe satisfies the whole gang. My kids love extra toppings, like Cheddar cheese and salsa, even though these tacos are great with just a little Spicy Avocado Cream.

Serves: 4
Prep time: 10 minutes
Cook time: 35 minutes

2 large boneless, skinless chicken breasts (about 1 pound total)

2 tablespoon chili powder

1 teaspoon seasoned salt

2 tablespoons olive oil

1 large onion, peeled, halved and thinly sliced

1 large red bell pepper, seeded and cut into 2-inch strips

8 taco-size flour tortillas

⅔ cup Spicy Avocado Cream (page 170)

Optional: shredded Cheddar cheese, Three-Minute Blender Salsa (page 168) or store-bought salsa

1. Sprinkle the chicken with the chili powder and seasoned salt on all sides. Heat the oil in a large skillet over medium-high heat.

2. Add the chicken to the pan and cook for 8 minutes per side, or until the chicken is golden brown. Set aside on a plate. The chicken will not yet be cooked all the way through.

3. Add the onion and pepper to the pan and cook for 5 minutes, or until the vegetables start to soften.

4. Cut the chicken into ½-inch slices and place it back in the pan with the onion and pepper. Reduce the heat to medium and cook for 10 more minutes, or until the chicken is cooked through and is no longer pink inside. Remove it from the pan and cut the chicken into bite-size pieces.

5. Warm the flour tortillas in the microwave for a few seconds, if desired. Spoon some avocado cream on each. Top with chicken. Serve with additional toppings, if desired.

Easy Variation: Substitute store-bought guacamole for the Spicy Avocado Cream to save even more time.

Spicy Turkey Sausage Marinara

DAIRY-FREE · FREEZER-FRIENDLY · GLUTEN-FREE · ONE POT/PAN

Growing up in a family that was part Italian, we called red sauce "gravy." Sunday gravy cooked all day and consisted of a big pot of sauce with sausage, pork ribs, and other meats bubbling away in it. This is my lightened-up and easy-to-cook version. It's so good with pasta, but rice or Italian bread works too.

Serves: 4
Prep time: 5 minutes
Cook time: 45 minutes

2 tablespoons olive oil

1 pound hot Italian turkey sausage links, cut into 2-inch pieces

3 garlic cloves, minced

½ cup red wine

1 (28-ounce) can crushed tomatoes

1 tablespoon dried basil

Salt

Red pepper flakes

1. In a large pot, heat the olive oil over medium-high heat and sauté the sausage for about 10 minutes, or until it starts to brown.

2. Turn the heat to medium. Add the garlic and cook for 3 minutes, or until slightly golden. Add the wine to deglaze pan. Stir in the tomatoes and basil.

3. Reduce the heat to low, cover, and simmer for 30 minutes, stirring occasionally. Add salt and red pepper to taste.

Leftovers: I make a double batch of this and keep half in the freezer. It freezes so well and is great for a quick weeknight dinner served with spaghetti. Freeze it in one-meal-size airtight containers. The night before you want to use it, put it in the refrigerator to defrost. When you're ready to eat, heat the sauce in a pot over medium heat and cook for 15 to 20 minutes, or until the sauce is simmering. Boil some pasta while the sausage marinara is cooking, and you have a nice, easy dinner.

Juicy Herb-Roasted Turkey Breast

DAIRY-FREE · GLUTEN-FREE · ONE POT/PAN

Turkey is not just for Thanksgiving! Roasting a turkey breast rather than a whole bird makes it easy enough to have turkey all year without much fuss. (If you do not have a big enough roasting pan, you can buy an inexpensive disposable one at the grocery store. This makes cleanup really easy, too.) Sometimes I cook a turkey breast on a Sunday night and we have delicious sandwiches for lunch all week. You can also use the leftovers to make a hearty turkey soup.

Serves: 6
Prep time: 5 minutes
Cook time: 1½ to 2 hours

1 (4- to 6-pound) turkey breast, skin on

1 tablespoon olive oil

1 tablespoon dry Italian seasoning

2 teaspoons seasoned salt

½ teaspoon black pepper

1 cup vegetable broth

1. Preheat the oven to 375°F. Lay the turkey breast in a roasting pan or large casserole dish and coat with the olive oil. Rub the skin with the Italian seasoning, pushing some under the skin. Sprinkle with the seasoned salt and pepper.

2. Pour the broth in the pan around the turkey breast.

3. Roast for 1½ to 2 hours. The turkey will be done when an instant-read thermometer inserted in the thickest part of the breast reads 165°F, or the turkey juices run clear and the meat is no longer pink.

4. Let the turkey rest for 15 minutes before slicing. Spoon the pan juices over the turkey, if desired.

Technique Tutorial: The easiest way to check to see if the turkey breast is done without having an instant-read thermometer is to cut a small slit in the thickest part of the breast. If the juices and meat are no longer pink, the turkey breast is ready to be taken out of the oven.

Mini Mexican Turkey Meatloaves

Meatloaf is a classic comfort food, and this one is lightened up by using ground turkey. Salsa and pepper jack cheese add some spice to your dinner. I love making mini meatloaves because they bake up much quicker than one big meatloaf.

Serves: 6
Prep time: 10 minutes
Cook time: 40 minutes

Nonstick cooking spray

1¼ pounds ground turkey

¾ cup seasoned breadcrumbs

½ teaspoon salt

1 egg, beaten

1 cup Three-Minute Blender Salsa (page 168), or store-bought salsa, divided

¾ cup shredded pepper jack cheese

1. Preheat the oven to 350°F. Spray a rimmed baking sheet with nonstick cooking spray.

2. In a large bowl, mix together the turkey, breadcrumbs, salt, egg, and ½ cup of the salsa. Form the mixture into 6 individual patties and place on the baking sheet.

3. Bake for 35 minutes, or until the turkey patties are cooked through and are no longer pink inside.

4. Remove from the oven and top with evenly divided amounts of the remaining ½ cup of salsa and cheese. Place back in the oven for about 5 minutes, or until the cheese is melted and bubbly.

Simple Swap: This recipe is also good using ground chicken or lean ground beef.

Turkey Sloppy Joes

30-MINUTE · FREEZER-FRIENDLY · GLUTEN-FREE · ONE POT/PAN

If you want a quick comfort food meal, sloppy joes are the way to go. I like using ground turkey because it's leaner than beef. Traditionally sloppy joes are served on hamburger buns, but I love to change things up a bit and serve them over rice or spaghetti. It's much less sloppy that way.

Serves: 4
Prep time: 5 minutes
Cook time: 25 minutes

1 tablespoon olive oil

1 pound ground turkey

1 (14-ounce) can diced tomatoes with onions and garlic

½ cup water

½ cup Basic BBQ Sauce (page 171), or store-bought barbecue sauce

¼ cup brown sugar

2 tablespoons tomato paste

1 teaspoon salt

Pinch of cayenne pepper

Buns or rolls, for serving

Optional: rice or spaghetti for serving (it's gluten-free only over rice)

1. In a large skillet, heat the oil on medium-high and cook the turkey for 3 to 5 minutes, or until it browns. Break it up with a wooden spoon as it cooks.

2. Add the tomatoes, water, barbecue sauce, brown sugar, and tomato paste. Cook on medium heat for a few minutes to bring to a simmer.

3. Reduce the heat to low and stir. Cover the pan and simmer for 10 minutes, stirring occasionally.

4. Uncover the pan and add salt and cayenne pepper to taste. Cook for about 5 more minutes uncovered, or until the sloppy joes get to your desired thickness. If the mixture gets too thick, you can always add a few extra spoonfuls of water.

5. Serve on buns, or with rice or spaghetti.

Technique Tutorial: To break up ground meat while it's cooking, so the meat will cook evenly and you won't end up with big clumps, use the back of a wooden spoon, and constantly turn the meat as it cooks. If you would like it more finely broken down, you can use a potato masher.

BBQ Turkey Meatballs

DAIRY-FREE · FREEZER-FRIENDLY · ONE POT/PAN

You can't go wrong with meatballs for dinner—or as an appetizer. I always keep a bag of these meatballs in my freezer. They are so easy to reheat and are great on rolls, or with mashed potatoes, rice, or pasta. Defrost them in your fridge overnight, then toss them in ¾ cup of barbecue sauce and heat in a casserole dish in a preheated 350°F oven for 20 to 30 minutes. If you are cooking them with marinara sauce, they can go frozen into a pot of heated sauce and then be cooked on medium to low heat for 20 to 30 minutes.

Serves: 4
Prep time: 15 minutes
Cook time: 30 minutes

1 pound ground turkey

1 egg, beaten

¾ cup seasoned breadcrumbs*

2 teaspoons dried parsley

½ teaspoon salt

¼ teaspoon black pepper

¾ cup plus 2 tablespoons Basic BBQ Sauce (page 171) or store-bought barbecue sauce, divided

*If you'd like to keep this recipe dairy-free, be sure to check that these don't contain cheese.

1. Preheat the oven to 350°F. Line a large rimmed baking sheet with parchment paper or aluminum foil. If using foil, spray with nonstick cooking spray.

2. In a large bowl, mix together the ground turkey, egg, breadcrumbs, parsley, salt, pepper, and 2 tablespoons of barbecue sauce. Mix until combined, then form into 12 golf-ball-size meatballs.

3. Place the meatballs on the baking sheet and bake for about 25 minutes, or until they are brown on the outside and no longer pink on the inside. If you're using an instant-read thermometer, it should be at 165°F. (If you are planning on freezing them, cool them down and place them in a plastic freezer bag in the freezer without the barbecue sauce.)

4. Toss the meatballs in a large bowl with the remaining ¾ cup of barbecue sauce. Place back in the pan and bake for 5 more minutes, or until the sauce on the meatballs is hot and bubbly.

Easy Variation: You can make these meatballs with Basic Marinara Sauce (page 173) or a store-bought sauce instead. Mix 2 tablespoons of marinara sauce with the turkey mixture. While the meatballs are baking, heat up 4 cups of marinara sauce over medium heat in a large pot. Bake the meatballs for 20 minutes, then transfer them to the pot of marinara sauce and cook for 5 more minutes on medium heat.

Chapter 11

Pork, Beef, and Lamb

Smoked Sausage and Sauerkraut Skillet

DAIRY-FREE · GLUTEN-FREE · ONE POT/PAN

This is an excellent dish to serve in the fall, during football season. It's one of my favorite game-day foods. It's great by itself next to some baked potatoes, but I like to also serve it as a sandwich on a roll with spicy mustard.

Serves: 6
Prep time: 5 minutes
Cook time: 30 minutes

2 tablespoons salted butter

1 large onion, peeled, halved, and thinly sliced

1 pound smoked sausage or smoked kielbasa, cut into 2-inch pieces

1½ cups hard cider

1 tablespoon sugar

1 (14-ounce) can sauerkraut, drained

1. Melt the butter in a large skillet over medium-high heat.

2. Add the onion and sauté for 3 minutes. Add the sausage to the pan and cook for another 5 minutes, or until the sausage starts to brown. Pour the hard cider into the pan.

3. Cook for 5 minutes, stirring occasionally, until the liquid starts to evaporate. Stir in the sugar, then add the drained sauerkraut. Bring to a simmer, then lower the heat to medium.

4. Cook for about 15 more minutes, or until most of the liquid evaporates.

Simple Swap: Hard cider is an alcoholic beverage similar to beer and can be found at the liquor store and at some supermarkets (depending on the laws in your state). You can use either apple or pear hard cider. If you'd prefer not to use alcohol, you can substitute apple juice, but then omit the sugar.

Sausage, Potato, and Pepper Sheet Pan Dinner

DAIRY-FREE · GLUTEN-FREE · ONE POT/PAN

This easy dinner is always a favorite in my house. I love the easy cleanup of sheet pan dinners. My husband prefers pork sausage, but to make this recipe a little leaner and lighter, I sometimes use chicken or turkey sausage.

Serves: 4
Prep time: 10 minutes
Cook time: 25 minutes

4 medium potatoes, peeled and cut into 2-inch cubes

1 large onion, peeled, halved, and thinly sliced

1 large red bell pepper, seeded and cut into 2-inch strips

1 tablespoon olive oil

1 teaspoon seasoned salt

1 pound (5 or 6) Italian sausage links

1. Preheat the oven to 400°F. Line a large rimmed baking sheet with parchment paper.

2. In a medium bowl, toss together the potatoes, onion, and bell pepper. Mix with the olive oil and sprinkle with the seasoned salt.

3. Arrange the vegetables evenly on the baking sheet and nestle the sausages into the vegetables.

4. Place the pan in the oven and roast for about 25 minutes, or until the sausages are completely cooked through and the potatoes are tender.

5. Slice the sausage links into pieces and serve mixed with the vegetables.

Leftovers: I like to chop up the leftovers into smaller pieces the next morning and fry them in a pan with a little butter or oil. They are great served for breakfast with a fried or scrambled egg on top.

Slow Cooker BBQ Pork Sliders

DAIRY-FREE · FREEZER-FRIENDLY · GLUTEN-FREE · ONE POT/PAN · SLOW COOKER

Several months ago, I went to North Carolina with my teenage son and we enjoyed some barbecue sandwiches. I knew I had to find a way to make these sandwiches at home, because I loved the vinegary sauce they use down South. While my husband is the barbecue guy in the family and cooks outside in our smoker, I found an easy way to make pork barbecue inside. I will be making these sliders using the slow cooker all year round.

Serves: 6
Prep time: 15 minutes
Cook time: 4 to 8 hours

---

1 (3-pound) boneless pork shoulder or butt roast

1 to 2 tablespoons barbecue seasoning or rub

¼ cup cider vinegar

1 cup Basic BBQ Sauce (page 171) or your favorite bottled brand, plus more for serving

12 slider rolls, sliced in half

24 pickle chips

1. Trim the excess fat from the pork roast and pat dry with paper towels. Rub it with the seasoning and place it in a heated slow cooker.

2. Combine the vinegar and barbecue sauce in a small bowl and pour it over the pork. Cover and cook on low for at least 4 hours, until the pork is fork-tender.

3. Remove the pork from the slow cooker and place in a large bowl. Use forks to shred the meat.

4. Discard half the juice in the slow cooker. Return the meat to the slow cooker and add extra barbecue sauce, if desired.

5. If you do not have a slow cooker, in a large pot on the stove, add 1 tablespoon olive oil. Brown the seasoned pork roast over medium heat, then add the vinegar, barbecue sauce, and ½ cup water. Bring the liquid to a simmer, cover, and cook on medium low for 2½ to 3 hours, or until the pork is tender and can be shredded with forks. If the liquid gets too thick or evaporates, add a little more water. Shred the pork as in step 3, and proceed with step 6.

6. Pile the shredded pork into the slider rolls. Serve with pickles and extra sauce on the side.

Prep Tip: This recipe serves 6, so you'll need a 3-pound pork roast because it will shrink quite a bit. Both a shoulder cut and a butt roast work. If you get one with the bone in, make sure it is larger, as you want to start with 3 pounds of meat. If you cannot find the size you need, you can also use 3 pounds of boneless country ribs. Since these are smaller cuts of meat, the slow cooking should take about 6 hours on low.

Hawaiian Ham Steaks

30-MINUTE · GLUTEN-FREE · ONE POT/PAN

My family loves ham, but cooking a whole one takes several hours and there is so much left over. A ham is great for the holidays, but not so great for a weeknight dinner. The simple solution is to cook these Hawaiian ham steaks. They take only 15 minutes, you cook only what you need, and everyone is happy.

Serves: 4
Prep time: 5 minutes
Cook time: 15 minutes

3 tablespoons butter, divided

2 (8-ounce) ham steaks

1 (20-ounce) can pineapple rings in natural juice, drained and juice reserved

2 tablespoons brown sugar

1 teaspoon spicy mustard

1. Melt 1 tablespoon of butter in a large skillet over medium-high heat. Add the ham steaks and cook for 2 to 3 minutes on each side, until the ham starts to brown. Transfer the ham steaks to a plate and keep warm.

2. Add the remaining 2 tablespoons of butter to the same skillet and turn the heat down to medium. Add 8 pineapple rings and cook for 1 to 2 minutes on each side, or until the pineapple slices are heated through. Remove from the pan and keep warm on the plate with the ham.

3. Add ½ cup of reserved pineapple juice, the brown sugar, and the mustard to the skillet. Whisk together and cook for 5 minutes, or until the sugar is dissolved and the sauce starts to thicken. You can add more pineapple juice if you want. Place the ham steaks back in the skillet and cook for approximately 5 more minutes with the sauce.

4. Cut the ham steaks in half and serve with the sauce and pineapple slices on top.

Simple Swap: You can substitute one large ham steak (1 to 1 ½ pounds) for the two smaller ones. Make sure to add a few extra minutes of cooking time when you're first adding the ham to the pan.

Easy Corned Beef and Cabbage Dinner

DAIRY-FREE · GLUTEN-FREE · ONE POT/PAN

Ever since I can remember, I've always eaten corned beef on St. Patrick's Day. This is an easy, no-stress meal to make. The leftover corned beef makes a great sandwich the next day, too.

Serves: 6
Prep time: 15 minutes
Cook time: 3 hours

1 (2- to 3-pound) corned beef brisket (with spice packet included)

3 large carrots, peeled and cut into 2-inch pieces

2 large onions, peeled and cut into quarters

1 small head cabbage, cut into 8 wedges

6 medium potatoes, peeled and quartered

1. Place the corned beef in a large pot. Cover with water. Add the spice packet contents to the water. Turn the heat on high and bring to a boil.

2. Reduce the heat to low and cover with a lid. Simmer for 2½ hours. Add the carrots, onions, cabbage, and potatoes. Cook on medium heat for 20 to 30 minutes more, or until the beef and vegetables are fork-tender.

3. Remove the corned beef and transfer to a cutting board. Cut the beef across the grain into ½-inch-thick slices. Drain the vegetables and serve with the beef.

Easy Variation: Substitute a 2- to 3-pound boneless ham for the corned beef. Since there will be no spice packet, add 1 teaspoon of black pepper to the water. The ham needs to cook for only 45 minutes in the first step, then another 20 to 30 minutes after the vegetables are added. By making a ham instead of corned beef, you will save more than an hour of cooking time.

Blue Cheese and Bacon Burgers

30-MINUTE · DAIRY-FREE · GLUTEN-FREE · ONE POT/PAN

There really is nothing like the smell of a sizzling burger right out of the pan. Blue cheese and bacon make these burgers even better. To make things easy, I use precooked bacon and microwave it according to the package instructions before using it to top my burgers.

Serves: 4
Prep time: 15 minutes
Cook time: 10 minutes

1½ pounds ground beef (80 percent lean)

1½ teaspoons seasoned salt

½ teaspoon black pepper

2 tablespoons canola oil

4 ounces blue cheese, crumbled

6 hamburger buns

6 precooked slices of bacon, microwaved and cut into pieces

1 large tomato, cut into 8 thin slices

1. In a medium bowl, combine the beef, seasoned salt, and black pepper. Mix gently with your hands until all the ingredients are combined.

2. Divide the beef mixture into 4 equal portions. Form each portion into a ½-inch-thick patty.

3. Heat the oil in a pan over medium-high heat. Place the burgers in the pan and cook for 3 to 4 minutes, or until the burgers are nicely seared on one side. Flip the patties and cook for 4 or 5 minutes on the other side, depending on how done you like them. Medium-cooked burgers usually take about 8 minutes total cooking time. For medium rare, cook for a little less time, while well done will take a few more minutes. Make a small slit with a knife to check on your burgers' doneness.

4. Add the cheese on top, dividing evenly among the burgers, then top each with 1½ slices of cooked bacon. Put a lid on the pan or tent the top with foil to melt the cheese.

5. Sandwich the four burgers between the buns, along with 2 slices of tomato for each bun. Serve immediately with any additional toppings you might like.

Simple Swap: Substitute any cheese you like for the blue cheese. My son is not a huge fan of blue cheese, so I make his with a sharp Cheddar. It goes great with these burgers as well.

Perfect Pan-Grilled Strip Steak

GLUTEN-FREE · ONE POT/PAN

This is my teenage son's favorite dinner. When I announce that we are having steak, both my husband's and son's eyes light up. The great thing is that steak is not hard to cook, and my son now makes the perfect one himself.

Serves: 4
Prep time: 35 minutes
Cook time: 15 minutes

---

2 (12-ounce) strip steaks, about 1½ inches thick

2 teaspoons steak seasoning

1 to 2 tablespoons canola oil

1 to 2 tablespoons Spreadable Herbed Butter (page 167)

1. Let the steaks sit at room temperature for 30 to 60 minutes. Then pat them with paper towels and sprinkle the seasoning on both sides of the steaks.

2. Preheat a large, heavy skillet to medium-high heat. Add just enough oil to coat the bottom of the pan and let it heat for 1 minute.

3. Add the steaks to the hot pan and cook for 5 minutes to get a good sear. Do not move the steaks around, as you want a nice crust to form. Flip the steaks over and cook for 4 to 7 more minutes, depending on the desired doneness and the thickness of the steak.

4. Remove the steaks from the pan and let them rest on a plate for 3 to 4 minutes.

5. Turn the heat off, add the desired amount of herb butter to the pan, and let it melt. Pour the butter over the steaks before serving.

Technique Tutorial: Most people like their steak cooked either medium rare or medium. Any more usually will make a steak tough. If you have an instant-read thermometer, here's a guide to steak doneness: rare, 130°F; medium rare, 135°F; medium, 140°F; medium well, 150°F. You insert the thermometer at the end of cooking. If you don't have a thermometer, you can cut a little nick into the steak to see how red it is. It is better to undercook than overcook, as you can always put the steak back in the pan for a few more minutes.

Slow Cooker Beef and Beer Mushroom Roast

DAIRY-FREE · SLOW COOKER

There is nothing better than the smell of a roast cooking in the slow cooker on a Sunday afternoon while you are watching a football game with the family. This flavorful roast, with mushrooms and beer, is perfect to serve with mashed potatoes or noodles. The gravy is on the thinner side, but you can always add a bit of flour during the last 30 minutes of cooking time, if you prefer it thicker. Just mix a few spoonfuls of flour with equal amounts of water until well blended, and stir into the gravy in the slow cooker.

Serves: 6
Prep time: 15 minutes
Cook time: 4 to 8 hours

---

1 (3-pound) beef round roast

1 tablespoon kosher salt, plus more if needed

2 teaspoons ground pepper, plus more if needed

3 tablespoons all-purpose flour

3 tablespoons canola oil

1½ cups beer

1 cup chopped onion

1 pound mushrooms, thickly sliced

1 tablespoon dried Italian seasoning

1. Heat a large frying pan over medium-high heat. Season the roast with the salt and pepper, then coat it with the flour. Add the oil to the pan and sear the roast for 6 to 8 minutes, turning it to brown on all sides. Remove the roast and place it in a preheated slow cooker.

2. Reduce heat in the pan to low, add the beer, and deglaze, scraping the bottom so the bits get mixed in. Stir the onion, mushrooms, and Italian seasoning into the pan and cook for a few minutes, until the vegetables start to soften. Pour the mixture over the roast.

3. Cover and cook on high for 4 to 6 hours or on low for 6 to 8 hours, until the roast is fork-tender. Season with extra salt and pepper, if needed.

4. If you don't have a slow cooker, after seasoning the roast, heat the oil in a large pot. Brown the roast, then add the beer, onion, mushrooms, and seasoning to the pot. Stir in 1 cup of water. Mix well, then cover and cook on low for about 3 hours, or until the roast is tender. Check the roast every half hour and spoon some of the juices over it. You might need to add more water. Season with salt and pepper to taste.

5. You can either slice or shred the meat, depending on how you like it. Cook it a little longer if you'd like to shred it. After removing the roast from the slow cooker or pot, stir the mushroom gravy well and serve it with the roast.

Ingredient Tip: When making pot roast in a slow cooker, I prefer round roasts because they are the leanest cuts of beef. If you use a lean cut, you won't have to worry about removing grease or fat at the end of cooking. Round roasts are sold as top round roasts or bottom round. I have used both to make pot roast. They are sold in the meat section, and you can always ask the butcher at your grocery store if you don't see it.

Easy Beef Bolognese Sauce

DAIRY-FREE · FREEZER-FRIENDLY · GLUTEN-FREE

Bolognese sauce is a meat-based sauce that originated in Bologna, Italy. It's the classic red meat sauce for spaghetti. There are plenty of versions out there that require more work than this recipe. But this one is easy, delicious, and company-worthy. Serve it over any type of pasta or rice. I love to serve it garnished with basil and grated cheese if it is going over pasta.

Serves: 6
Prep time: 5 minutes
Cook time: 45 minutes

---

1 tablespoon olive oil

⅓ cup finely chopped onion

1 tablespoon crushed or minced garlic

1 pound lean ground beef

1 tablespoon dried Italian seasoning

1 tablespoon onion powder

1 (28-ounce) can crushed tomatoes

½ cup red wine

Salt

Black pepper

1. Heat the olive oil over medium-high heat in a large pot. Add the onion and sauté for 5 minutes, or until translucent. Add the garlic and sauté for another 3 minutes, or until it becomes fragrant.

2. Add the ground beef and stir with a wooden spoon to break it up. Cook for 5 minutes, or until it starts to brown.

3. Add the Italian seasoning, onion powder, tomatoes, and wine. Stir well and turn the heat to low.

4. Cover the pot and simmer on low for 30 minutes, stirring occasionally, until the sauce is thick. Season with salt and pepper to taste.

Technique Tutorial: The onion and garlic are sautéed to break them down quickly and give lots of flavor to this sauce. Garlic can burn quickly, so make sure to keep an eye on it as you cook.

Balsamic Rosemary Lamb Chops

30-MINUTE · DAIRY-FREE · GLUTEN-FREE · ONE POT/PAN

I love making lamb chops when company comes over or as a special dinner for my family. They are quite easy to make and take very little time. These lamb chops are perfect next to roasted or mashed potatoes and a simple fresh salad. This recipe is one of my husband's favorites.

Serves: 4
Prep time: 5 minutes
Cook time: 15 minutes

8 loin lamb chops (about 2 pounds total)

1 teaspoon seasoned salt

½ teaspoon black pepper

1 teaspoon dried rosemary

2 tablespoons olive oil

¼ cup balsamic vinegar

1 tablespoon honey

1 to 2 tablespoons Spreadable Herbed Butter (page 167) or plain salted butter

1. Sprinkle the lamb chops with the seasoned salt, pepper, and rosemary.

2. Heat a large frying pan over medium-high heat. Add the oil to the pan, then add the lamb chops. Cook the chops 4 to 5 minutes on each side, or until they reach the desired doneness. Transfer to a plate and loosely cover with aluminum foil.

3. Add the vinegar and honey to the pan and stir to deglaze, making sure you get all the browned bits mixed in. Cook for 3 to 5 minutes on low heat, or until the sauce is starting to thicken. Stir in the desired amount of herbed butter and mix well.

4. Put the lamb chops back in the pan and spoon the sauce over them. Serve hot.

Ingredient Tip: When buying lamb chops, I always get the loin ones. They are not as pretty as rib chops, but are usually less expensive and more meaty. I find them just as tasty but a much better value.

Chapter 12

Desserts

Chocolate Mousse Cheesecake Dessert Dip

30-MINUTE · GLUTEN-FREE · NO-COOK · VEGETARIAN

One of my favorite local diners has a bakery that my family loves. They have the best chocolate mousse cheesecake, and it's always a hit on birthdays and special occasions. I made this dessert dip because it reminds me of that decadent cheesecake. It's the perfect party dessert, and once you make it, your friends and family will ask for it all the time.

Serves: 8 to 10

Prep time: 10 minutes, plus 10 minutes to chill

¾ cup Fuss-Free Chocolate Syrup (page 175)

8 ounces cream cheese, softened

½ cup heavy cream

Optional: strawberries or other fresh fruit, pretzels and/or graham crackers (in which case the dish will not be gluten-free)

1. In a medium bowl, beat together the chocolate syrup and cream cheese with an electric hand mixer on low speed until well blended.

2. Add the cream and beat the mixture on low speed until it's smooth and creamy.

3. Put the mixture into a serving bowl and chill for at least 10 minutes (it can be chilled overnight if you want to make it in advance).

4. Serve with fresh fruit slices, pretzels, and/or graham crackers.

Easy Variation: You can substitute store-bought fudge or sundae sauce for the Fuss-Free Chocolate Syrup. You'll find it in the ice cream topping isle at your grocery store.

Microwave Peanut Butter S'mores

30-MINUTE · VEGETARIAN

In the summer, my family always looks forward to toasting marshmallows on the fire pit to make s'mores. We decided this should not be just a summer affair, and now make them indoors all year long. I've added some peanut butter to make them even more delicious.

Serves: 4
Prep time: 5 minutes
Cook time: 15 seconds

4 graham crackers, neatly broken in half

4 teaspoons peanut butter

4 mini chocolate bars

4 marshmallows, halved

1. Place 4 halves of the graham crackers on a microwave-safe plate.

2. Spread 1 teaspoon of peanut butter on each graham cracker half, then top each with a mini chocolate bar and 2 marshmallow halves.

3. Microwave the s'mores for 15 seconds, or until the marshmallows slightly expand as they heat.

4. Remove the plate from the microwave and top each s'more with another graham cracker half, pressing down to form a sandwich.

Simple Swap: Swap cookie butter for peanut butter and you will have a very sweet treat!

Best-Ever Brownies

These brownies are crackly on the outside and chewy on the inside, just the way my family likes them, and my kids constantly ask me to make them. They use only five ingredients, so why use a boxed mix when you can bake these? When there are leftovers, they are perfect to wrap up and put in lunch boxes.

Makes: 12 brownies
Prep time: 10 minutes
Cook time: 25 minutes, plus 20 minutes to cool

Nonstick cooking spray

1 cup all-purpose flour

1 cup sugar

½ cup unsweetened cocoa powder

½ cup salted butter, melted

2 large eggs

Optional: powdered sugar

1. Preheat the oven to 350°F. Line an 8- or 9-inch square baking pan with enough foil so it comes up above the edges of the pan. Lightly coat the foil with nonstick cooking spray.

2. In a medium bowl, whisk together the flour, sugar, and cocoa powder.

3. In a small bowl, whisk together the butter and the eggs. Add the egg mixture to the flour mixture, stirring until well combined.

4. Spread the batter evenly in the foil-lined pan.

5. Bake the brownies for 20 to 25 minutes, or until a toothpick inserted in the center comes out clean. Using the foil, lift the brownies out of the pan and place on a cutting board to cool. Cool for 20 minutes before cutting the brownies into 12 squares. Sprinkle with some powdered sugar, if desired.

Technique Tutorial: To line the baking pan with foil, use a square that has been cut larger than the pan so you can use the edges as handles to lift out the brownies. This makes it easy to cool the brownies and even easier to clean the pan. I like to refrigerate my brownies for half an hour after they cool to room temperature, because it gives them a moist texture and makes them easier to cut.

Layered Brownie Sundaes

30-MINUTE · NO-COOK · VEGETARIAN

While everyone loves sundaes, brownie sundaes are even better! These are made with homemade brownies and layered with vanilla ice cream topped with whipped cream. Feel free to use any flavor of ice cream you like, and don't forget to top everything with cherries.

Serves: 4
Prep time: 10 minutes

8 large scoops vanilla ice cream

4 Best-Ever Brownies (page 154)

¼ to ½ cup Fuss-Free Chocolate Syrup (page 175)

1 cup Homemade Whipped Cream (page 174)

4 Maraschino cherries

1. Put 1 scoop of ice cream into each of 4 dessert bowls or parfait dishes. Place 1 brownie over each scoop of ice cream, then top with a second scoop of ice cream. Pour the desired amount of chocolate syrup over the ice cream.

2. Garnish with whipped cream and a cherry.

Easy Variation: While I like to make brownies and keep homemade chocolate syrup and homemade whipped cream in the fridge when I can, feel free to use store-bought brownies and chocolate sauce to save time. Canned whipped cream is great in a pinch, too.

Funfetti Sugar Cookies

30-MINUTE · FREEZER-FRIENDLY · ONE POT/PAN · VEGETARIAN

These cookies look and taste like they came from a bakery. I love to add sprinkles based on the season—red, yellow, and orange in the fall, pink in the spring, and so on. You most likely have all the ingredients you need to make them right now.

Makes: 12 cookies
Prep time: 10 minutes
Cook time: 15 minutes

6 tablespoons salted butter, softened

½ cup sugar

1 large egg

1¼ cups all-purpose flour

¼ cup colored sprinkles

1. Preheat the oven to 350°F. Line a large rimmed baking sheet with parchment paper.

2. In a medium mixing bowl, use an electric hand mixer to beat together the butter and sugar on high speed for 1 minute, or until well blended. Add the egg and beat on high speed for 2 minutes, until the batter is fluffy and smooth.

3. Slowly add in the flour and mix on low speed until blended. Do not overmix.

4. Gently mix in the sprinkles using a rubber spatula.

5. Drop tablespoonfuls of cookie dough onto the baking sheet, leaving 1 to 2 inches of space between each one. You should get about 12 cookies from the dough.

6. Bake for 9 to 12 minutes or until the edges are set. Cool for 5 minutes, then set the cookies on a cooling rack or sheet of wax paper. Cool for 10 more minutes before serving.

7. Store leftovers in an airtight container.

Leftovers: Baked cookies can be frozen for several months. Cool the cookies to room temperature, then place them on a baking sheet in the freezer until they're frozen solid. Transfer to an airtight bag or container. To defrost, take them out of the bag and let them sit out at room temperature for about an hour, or until they are no longer frozen. You can also place them frozen on a baking sheet in a preheated 300°F oven for about 10 minutes, or until they are defrosted and warm. They will taste like they just came from a bakery oven!

Concord Grape Thumbprint Cookies

I have loved the smell of Concord grapes ever since I was a kid and my grandfather grew them. Since Concord grape season is a short one in the fall, I don't get the opportunity to smell them often. The next best thing is to bake these cookies. They smell wonderful while baking and will melt in your mouth.

Makes: About 16 cookies
Prep time: 10 minutes, plus 1 hour to chill
Cook time: 30 minutes

½ cup salted butter

⅓ cup sugar

1 cup all-purpose flour

2 to 3 tablespoons Concord grape jam

2 to 3 tablespoons powdered sugar

1. Using an electric hand mixer, beat the butter and sugar together on low speed until creamy. Gradually add the flour until the dough becomes crumbly. Using your hands or a wooden spoon, mix the dough so that it forms a large ball. Wrap the ball of dough in plastic wrap and refrigerate for at least 1 hour.

2. Preheat the oven to 350°F. Line a large rimmed baking sheet with parchment paper.

3. Pull pieces off the dough with your hands and roll them into 1-inch balls. Place the balls 1 inch apart on the baking sheet.

4. Using your thumb, make an indentation in the middle of each dough ball and flatten the cookie so that there is a nice little well. Fill each with about ¼ to ½ teaspoon of jam, making sure not to overfill.

5. Bake for 13 to 16 minutes, or until the edges of the cookies start to turn golden brown. Remove from the oven and cool for 20 minutes.

6. Sprinkle with a dusting of powdered sugar before serving.

Simple Swap: Substitute any flavor of jam for grape. You could even use more than one flavor in the same batch of cookies.

Grilled Peaches and Cream

30-MINUTE · GLUTEN-FREE · ONE POT/PAN · VEGETARIAN

I make this easy dessert when peaches are at peak season in New Jersey. They are really wonderful to serve to company. To make this dessert even more decadent, try serving them with some vanilla ice cream.

Serves: 4
Prep time: 5 minutes
Cook time: 10 minutes

---

2 tablespoons butter

4 ripe peaches, halved and pitted

4 tablespoons light brown sugar

1 cup Homemade Whipped Cream (page 174), or canned whipped cream or whipped topping

¼ cup finely chopped toasted pecans

1. Melt the butter on medium heat in a large frying pan. Place the peaches in the pan cut-side down and grill for 4 to 5 minutes, or until they start to soften. Turn the peaches over and sprinkle with brown sugar. Cook for 5 more minutes, or until the peaches are tender and juicy.

2. Place the peach halves on a platter and top each with some whipped cream. Sprinkle with the chopped pecans.

Simple Swap: To lighten up this recipe, substitute low-fat vanilla Greek yogurt for the whipped cream.

Apple Bread Pudding

ONE POT/PAN · VEGETARIAN

Bread pudding has always reminded me of the holidays because it's such a special dessert. This bread pudding can be made in advance and then heated right before serving. To make it even more decadent than it already is, serve it topped with Homemade Whipped Cream (page 174) or vanilla ice cream.

Serves: 9
Prep time: 20 minutes
Cook time: 55 minutes

2 cups half-and-half or light cream

½ cup sugar, plus 2 tablespoons

1 teaspoon cinnamon

3 eggs, beaten

Nonstick cooking spray

8 slices white or potato bread, cut into small cubes

2 medium apples, peeled, cored, and chopped

1. Preheat the oven to 350°F.

2. In a medium bowl, whisk together the half-and-half, ½ cup of sugar, the cinnamon, and the eggs.

3. Spray an 8- to 10-inch square baking pan or medium casserole dish with nonstick cooking spray. Put the bread and apples in it and mix together thoroughly. Pour the cream mixture over the top and let sit for 5 minutes so the bread absorbs the liquid.

4. Bake for 30 minutes, then remove from the oven and sprinkle the remaining 2 tablespoons of sugar on top. Place the pan back in the oven.

5. Bake for 20 to 25 minutes more, or until a knife inserted in the center comes out nearly clean and the top is golden brown.

Leftovers: This bread pudding can be made a day in advance and stored in the refrigerator. Reheat it in a 350°F oven for 10 minutes, or longer if you like it warmer. It makes 9 servings, so if there are leftovers, individual pieces can be reheated in the microwave for about 30 seconds.

Easy Key Lime Pie

ONE POT/PAN · VEGETARIAN

There is nothing like a tart but sweet, creamy piece of pie. When my family vacationed in the Florida Keys, we made sure to try as many key lime pies as possible, and they were all amazing. This recipe requires some chilling time in the refrigerator, but it takes only about 20 minutes to make.

Serves: 6 to 8
Prep time: 10 minutes, plus 4 hours to chill
Cook time: 15 minutes

1 (14-ounce) can sweetened condensed milk

3 egg yolks

½ cup lime juice

1 (6-ounce) prebaked graham cracker crust

1 cup Homemade Whipped Cream (page 174), or whipped topping or canned whipped cream

1. Preheat the oven to 350°F.

2. In a medium bowl, whisk together the condensed milk, egg yolks, and lime juice. Pour into the prebaked crust and bake for about 12 minutes.

3. Let the pie cool for 15 minutes before chilling in the refrigerator. Refrigerate for at least 4 hours before serving.

4. Top with whipped cream right before serving.

Technique Tutorial: To separate egg yolks from the whites, rest a slotted spoon over a bowl and crack the egg into it. Very gently shake the spoon from side to side so that the whites fall through the slots and into the bowl. Store the egg whites in an airtight container in the fridge to add to omelets or scrambled eggs.

Cinnamon Pear Cream Cheese Tart

ONE POT/PAN · VEGETARIAN

Frozen puff pastry dough is easy to use, but everyone will think you spent hours making this elegant dessert. Find it in the freezer section of your grocery store. It comes in a package of two folded sheets to a box. I love having leftovers for breakfast the next morning; individual pieces can be heated in the microwave for 20 or 30 seconds. If you prefer apples, they can easily be substituted for pears.

Serves: 6 to 8
Prep time: 15 minutes, plus 30 minutes to defrost
Cook time: 20 minutes

---

2 pears, peeled, cored, and cut into long, thin slices

½ cup plus 2 tablespoons sugar, divided

1 large sheet (8 to 9 ounces) frozen puff pastry

4 ounces cream cheese, softened

½ teaspoon cinnamon

1. Mix the pears with 2 tablespoons of sugar in a medium bowl. Set aside for 30 minutes while the puff pastry is defrosting on the counter.

2. Preheat the oven to 400°F. Line a large rimmed baking sheet with parchment paper.

3. Unfold the pastry sheet and place it on the prepared baking sheet. Roll it out so that it's a few inches bigger all around.

4. In a small bowl, beat together the cream cheese and ½ cup sugar, either by hand or using an electric hand mixer. Gently spread the cream cheese mixture on the pastry dough.

5. Drain any liquid from the pears and place the slices on top of the cream cheese in neat, overlapping rows, leaving ½ inch all around the outer edges of the pastry sheet. Sprinkle with the cinnamon.

6. Bake the tart for 16 to 20 minutes, or until the edges of the pastry are golden brown.

7. Cool for at least 15 minutes before serving.

Technique Tutorial: The best way to roll out pastry dough is using a rolling pin. If you don't have one, a tall drinking glass or wine bottle will do the trick.

Chapter 13

Sauces, Dressings, and Staples

Simple Italian Vinaigrette or Marinade

Making your own salad dressing is easy and tastes so good. During the summer, I frequently add chopped fresh herbs, such as basil, parsley, or cilantro, to my dressing. Change things up a bit and substitute another fresh herb for the Italian seasoning. This dressing will keep well in the fridge for up to several weeks with dried herbs, but if you use fresh herbs, make sure to use it within 2 to 3 days.

Makes: About 1¼ cups

Prep time: 5 minutes

¼ cup cider vinegar or red wine vinegar

¾ cup olive oil

3 tablespoons water

1 teaspoon dried Italian seasoning

½ teaspoon garlic powder

2 tablespoons sugar

Salt

Black pepper

1. Add the vinegar, olive oil, water, Italian seasoning, garlic powder, and sugar to a blender. Blend for 30 seconds or until emulsified.

2. Season with salt and pepper to taste.

Easy Variation: You can put the dressing in a mason jar with a tight lid and shake until well blended. Or put all the ingredients in a small bowl and whisk until they're emulsified.

Spreadable Herbed Butter

30-MINUTE · GLUTEN-FREE · NO-COOK · VEGETARIAN

I love the texture of butter that has been sitting out on the counter for a while. This butter has that same creamy texture right out of the refrigerator. The dried herbs and garlic powder give it great flavor to spread on bread, or add a pat to your steak or chicken.

Makes: 1½ cups butter
Prep time: 5 minutes

1 cup salted butter, softened

½ cup olive oil

1½ teaspoons dried Italian seasoning

1 teaspoon garlic powder

¼ teaspoon salt

1. Add all the ingredients to a blender. Blend together on medium speed until smooth. Or you could beat the butter with a electric hand mixer in a medium bowl.

2. Scrape the butter with a spatula into an airtight container and refrigerate until ready to use. This will keep in the fridge for 3 weeks. If you won't use it all by then, the recipe can be halved (just make it with half of all the ingredients).

Simple Swap: Substitute 1 teaspoon of crumbled dried rosemary for the Italian seasoning to give your butter a bit of a different flavor.

Three-Minute Blender Salsa

This salsa is so easy to put together, but tastes like something you'd get in a Mexican restaurant. It's the perfect condiment for tacos, burgers, or grilled chicken. Serve it with corn tortilla chips and you have a nice gluten-free appetizer or snack. Store this salsa in an airtight container in the refrigerator for 4 to 5 days. You can also freeze it and defrost it in the fridge the night before you want to serve it.

Makes: About 4 cups

Prep time: 3 minutes

2 (14-ounce) cans fire-roasted tomatoes

1 poblano pepper, seeded and chopped

⅓ cup chopped onion

⅓ cup packed fresh cilantro

Juice of 1 lime

Sea salt

Black pepper

1. Put the tomatoes, poblano pepper, onion, cilantro, and lime juice into a blender. Blend for 1 to 2 minutes, until smooth. You can also make the salsa in a bowl using an immersion blender.

2. Season with salt and pepper to taste.

Simple Swap: Poblano peppers have medium heat, but feel free to substitute 2 jalapeño peppers if you can't find poblanos or would like a little more heat.

Spicy Avocado Cream

30-MINUTE · GLUTEN-FREE · NO-COOK · VEGETARIAN

I put this avocado cream on tacos, burritos, and grilled chicken. My husband likes to dip tortilla chips in it, too. It's so good, you could eat it right out of the bowl with a spoon!

Makes: About 3 cups

Prep time: 10 minutes

2 avocados, peeled and pitted

16 ounces sour cream

Juice of 1 lime

1 teaspoon garlic powder

Salt

Cayenne pepper

1. In a medium bowl, mash the avocados.

2. Add the sour cream, lime juice, and garlic powder. Mix together well.

3. Season with salt and cayenne pepper to taste.

Leftovers: Keep the leftover avocado cream in an airtight container in the refrigerator for no more than 2 days. I like to use this as a salad dressing, too, so I make a big batch the day before I need it.

Basic BBQ Sauce

30-MINUTE · DAIRY-FREE · GLUTEN-FREE · ONE POT/PAN · VEGETARIAN

Making homemade barbecue sauce is great because you can control what goes into it. While there are several store-bought brands I like, nothing beats my own. Feel free to add a little less or more sugar, salt, or hot sauce so you can make this barbecue sauce exactly to your own taste.

Makes: About 2 cups
Prep time: 5 minutes
Cook time: 10 minutes

1½ cups ketchup

¼ cup packed light brown sugar

2 tablespoons cider vinegar

1 teaspoon seasoned salt

1 teaspoon garlic powder

1 teaspoon chili powder

¼ cup water

1. In a small saucepan, whisk together all the ingredients.

2. Heat the pan over medium heat and cook the sauce for 5 minutes, or until it comes to a simmer. Cook for 10 more minutes, or until you get your desired thickness.

3. Cool before storing in an airtight container in the refrigerator for up to 1 week.

Ingredient Tip: If the brown sugar gets hard and stuck together in the pantry, you can soften it up by microwaving it. Put it in a microwavable bowl with a wet paper towel on top. Microwave in 20-second increments until the sugar is soft.

10-Minute Gravy

30-MINUTE · FREEZER-FRIENDLY · ONE POT/PAN · VEGETARIAN

Why buy jarred gravy when you can make it in 10 minutes? The great thing about this gravy is that you can use whatever broth you choose. If you use vegetable broth, it is a perfect vegetarian gravy recipe.

Makes: About 1 cup
Prep time: 5 minutes
Cook time: 10 minutes

2 tablespoons butter

2 tablespoons flour

1 cup broth (beef, chicken, vegetable, or turkey), or more if needed

Salt

Black pepper

1. Melt the butter over medium-high heat in a small saucepan. Stir in the flour and mix into a thick paste. Pour in the broth and whisk vigorously until well combined. Reduce the heat to low.

2. Continue to cook for 3 to 5 minutes, stirring occasionally, until thickened. The gravy will be done when it is thick enough to coat the back of a spoon. If it gets too thick, add a little extra broth to thin it.

3. Season with salt and pepper to taste.

Leftovers: I like to make gravy in advance for holiday dinners. Gravy can be refrigerated for two days ahead of time, or put in the freezer for up to a month. To reheat gravy, put it in a saucepan and cook on medium heat until it's bubbling.

Basic Marinara Sauce

DAIRY-FREE · FREEZER-FRIENDLY · GLUTEN-FREE · VEGETARIAN

Marinara sauce is a staple in our house. On busy nights, I just pull some out of the freezer and serve it with ravioli, tortellini, or spaghetti. This versatile sauce also finds its way into soups, casseroles, and stews in my kitchen.

Makes: About 3½ cups
Prep time: 5 minutes
Cook time: 25 minutes

1 tablespoon olive oil

1 tablespoon crushed or minced garlic

1 (28-ounce) can crushed tomatoes with basil

1 tablespoon sugar

1 tablespoon dried Italian seasoning

Salt

Black pepper

Optional: 2 tablespoons chopped fresh basil leaves

1. Heat the olive oil over medium heat in a medium saucepan. Add the garlic and sauté for 2 minutes, or until lightly translucent.

2. Add the tomatoes, sugar, and Italian seasoning to the pot and stir well. Cover and simmer on low heat for 25 minutes.

3. Season with salt and pepper to taste. Stir in the fresh basil, if using.

Leftovers: Store leftover sauce in an airtight container in the refrigerator. You can also double the recipe and store this sauce in the freezer until you need to use it. It can then be defrosted in your refrigerator overnight and heated over medium heat in a medium saucepan for about 10 to 15 minutes.

Homemade Whipped Cream

There is nothing better than homemade whipped cream. I always keep a pint of cream in my refrigerator to whip up to make quick desserts. This goes perfectly on fresh berries, or for a real treat, add some to your morning coffee. To add a little different flavor to your whipped cream, swap almond or coffee extract for the vanilla. Actually, you can use almost any extract you'd like.

Makes: 2 cups
Prep time: 20 minutes

1 pint whipping cream

¼ cup powdered sugar

1 teaspoon vanilla

1. Place a medium mixing bowl in the freezer for 10 to 15 minutes, or until it starts to feel cold.

2. Pour the cream, sugar, and vanilla into the chilled bowl.

3. Using an electric hand mixer, beat the mixture on high speed for 1 to 2 minutes, or until it begins to form medium to stiff peaks.

4. Store in the refrigerator for no more than 2 or 3 days.

Technique Tutorial: When whipping cream, it's done when medium to stiff peaks form on the surface of the cream as you pull up the beaters. At this stage, dollops of the cream will have a pointy top. Do not overmix cream, because after the stiff-peak stage, it will turn to butter.

Fuss-Free Chocolate Syrup

30-MINUTE · DAIRY-FREE · GLUTEN-FREE · ONE POT/PAN · VEGETARIAN

My teenage son drinks gallons of chocolate milk every week. We go through so much chocolate syrup that I decided to make a homemade version, so I know exactly what ingredients and how much sugar are in it. This is perfect for making chocolate milk but is also a good topping for ice cream or to dip fruit in.

Makes: About 1 cup
Prep time: 5 minutes
Cook time: 10 minutes

½ cup unsweetened cocoa powder

¾ cup sugar

½ cup water

1 teaspoon vanilla

1. In a small saucepan, whisk together the cocoa powder and sugar. Add the water and vanilla. Mix well.

2. Place the saucepan over medium heat and bring the mixture to a boil, stirring constantly. Reduce the heat to low and simmer for about 3 more minutes, stirring to get a smooth consistency.

3. Remove from the heat and cool.

Leftovers: Store the leftovers in the refrigerator in an airtight container. The syrup will thicken a little as it chills. Make a double or triple batch, because this chocolate syrup can be stored in the refrigerator for up to 3 months.

MEASUREMENTS AND CONVERSIONS

VOLUME EQUIVALENTS (LIQUID)

US Standard	US Standard (ounces)	Metric (approximate)
2 tablespoons	1 fl. oz.	30 mL
¼ cup	2 fl. oz.	60 mL
½ cup	4 fl. oz.	120 mL
1 cup	8 fl. oz.	240 mL
1½ cups	12 fl. oz.	355 mL
2 cups or 1 pint	16 fl. oz.	475 mL
4 cups or 1 quart	32 fl. oz.	1 L
1 gallon	128 fl. oz.	4 L

OVEN TEMPERATURES

Fahrenheit (F)	Celsius (C) (approximate)
250°F	120°C
300°F	150°C
325°F	165°C
350°F	180°C
375°F	190°C
400°F	200°C
425°F	220°C
450°F	230°C

VOLUME EQUIVALENTS (DRY)

US Standard	Metric (approximate)
⅛ teaspoon	0.5 mL
¼ teaspoon	1 mL
½ teaspoon	2 mL
¾ teaspoon	4 mL
1 teaspoon	5 mL
1 tablespoon	15 mL
¼ cup	59 mL
⅓ cup	79 mL
½ cup	118 mL
⅔ cup	156 mL
¾ cup	177 mL
1 cup	235 mL
2 cups or 1 pint	475 mL
3 cups	700 mL
4 cups or 1 quart	1 L

WEIGHT EQUIVALENTS

US Standard	Metric (approximate)
½ ounce	15 g
1 ounce	30 g
2 ounces	60 g
4 ounces	115 g
8 ounces	225 g
12 ounces	340 g
16 ounces or 1 pound	455 g

GLOSSARY

al dente: Italian for "to the bite," food that is cooked to be firm; pasta is frequently cooked this way

aromatics: Fresh ingredients that add aroma and flavor, such as garlic, ginger root, and fresh herbs

baste: To pour juices or fat over meat to keep it moist and flavorful

braise: To cook first by browning, then covered over low heat in a small amount of liquid; most stews are braised, as this cooking process gives food lots of flavor

bubbling: When a pot of sauce or water comes to a boil and you see bubbles at the surface

caramelize: The process of browning sugar, resulting in a sweet nutty flavor; both fruits and vegetables will caramelize if cooked on high heat, due to their natural sugars

deglaze: Adding a liquid to a pan to remove browned food residue and incorporate it into the sauce, for flavor

dice: To cut food into small cubes that are uniform in size, typically, ⅛ inch wide to ¾ inch wide

emulsified: When two liquids are combined to form a smooth mixture

garnish: Something added to the top of a finished dish for visual appeal

grate: To reduce food to small shreds

marinate: To soak food in a seasoned liquid (the marinade) that often includes an acidic element, to tenderize or give it extra flavor

mince: To cut food into very small pieces, usually so it can be dissolved when cooking; garlic, herbs and other aromatics are often minced

packed: When the measuring cup or spoon is filled to the top, and then the ingredient is pushed down and you add a bit more to top it up; often done with brown sugar and chopped fresh herbs

purée: To blend food so that it turns into a paste

sauté: To cook food in a pan over relatively high heat with a small amount of fat; similar to panfrying, except the heat is a bit higher because the pieces of food are smaller and cook faster

sear: To cook food at intense heat so that a crust is formed; seals in the flavor and the juices of meats, poultry, and seafood

shred: To tear into long, narrow pieces

shuck: To remove the hard outer cover of food such as corn and shellfish

simmer: To cook slowly over low heat just below the boiling point; you will start to see small bubbles

softened: When foods like butter and cream cheese are taken out of the refrigerator and brought to room temperature

"to taste": As much or little of an ingredient as you would like

vacuum sealed: Food packaging that has had all the air taken out of it to keep it fresh longer

whisk: To beat or stir with a light, rapid movement; also a kitchen tool that does this

RECIPE INDEX

INDEX

ACKNOWLEDGMENTS

To my husband, daughter, and son: Thank you for always supporting me in the kitchen and in life. Whether it was testing my recipes, cleaning up the big messes, or tasting something I cooked, you guys did it all and are the best!

To my mother, father, and grandparents: Thank you for getting me interested in food at a very young age. Although my dad and grandparents are no longer physically on this earth, I am constantly reminded and inspired by the food memories I have of them.

To my friend Jodie, who doesn't love to cook like I do: Thanks for testing my recipes and being my taster and cheerleader.

To my neighbor Frank: Thank you for testing recipes at the drop of a dime and for always bringing me great foodie gifts from your travels.

To my friend Kristin: Thank you for your recipe testing, technical wisdom, and for being the best food blogger travel buddy.

To my cooking friend Jannine: Thanks for being a positive inspiration. Whenever I'm down or feel overwhelmed, I think of you and how anything can be overcome with a positive attitude.

To all my friends, family, and blog readers: Thanks for all your support. My blog would never be here without you.

To Elizabeth, Katie, Vanessa, and the Callisto Media team: I am so happy and grateful I was given this opportunity, and I couldn't have worked with a better group of people.

ABOUT THE AUTHOR

Lisa Grant is a mom, wife, dog owner, and food lover. She lives in southern New Jersey and is the creator of the blog Jersey Girl Cooks (www.jerseygirlcooks.com). While she loves to travel, her kitchen is still her favorite place in the world. When she's not in the kitchen, she can be found exploring cities with her college-age daughter, watching her teenage son's soccer games with her husband, or trying new restaurants with family and friends. You can find her @JerseyGirlCooks on Twitter, Instagram, and Facebook.

CPSIA information can be obtained
at www.ICGtesting.com
Printed in the USA
LVHW070139211218
601302LV00027B/770/P